Favourite Walks
in the
West Midlands

by
**Members of
Birmingham C.H.A. Rambling Club**

Edited by
Tom Birch and Mary Wall

Photography: Alf Gray

Word Processing: Gill Bunney

Maps: Mary Wall

Sales Manager: Joan Mensing

MERIDIAN BOOKS

Published 1994 by Meridian Books
© Birmingham CHA Rambling Club 1994

ISBN 1-869922-26-3

Meridian Books
40 Hadzor Road
Oldbury
Warley
West Midlands
B68 9LA

Printed in Great Britain by BPC Wheatons Ltd., Exeter.

Contents

Preface

AS A THANKSGIVING for all the pleasure that walking has given them over the years, the Birmingham C.H.A. Rambling Club members decided to celebrate their Ninetieth Anniversary by compiling this book of walks and give all the royalties to charity.

We hope that you enjoy the rambles as much as the contributors had in their preparation.

If you would like to walk with a friendly group why not join us? We have many varied walks, on weekdays and weekends, using public transport, cars and coaches.

You can obtain up-to-date information regarding the current rambles programme, and the name and location of the Membership Secretary from local libraries.

June Buckton

Chairman. Birmingham C.H.A. Rambling Club.

Members of Birmingham C.H.A. enjoying tea at Catherine de Barnes, Solihull after a ramble on June 7th. 1913.

Rambling in the Early Days of the Birmingham C.H.A.

by Harold Turner

THE BIRMINGHAM C.H.A. RAMBLING CLUB owes its origin to the initiative of two brothers, Tom and Arthur Hales, who while on holiday with the C.H.A. learnt from one of the other guests that rambling clubs had been formed in their towns by members of the C.H.A. who wished to keep the holiday spirit alive through the winter months until it was possible to arrange their next year's holiday. With the help of Head Office, members of the Midlands area were circularised and the first rambles were arranged. And so in 1904 the Club was born.

It appears to have been well organised from the very beginning, with a map library of six-inch maps mounted on linen and printed on the cover with the Club's full title. They covered the area of the countryside around Birmingham as far as would be reached on a Saturday afternoon's walk and were essential equipment for the Club's leaders.

In those days footpaths were not signposted, except in rare cases, and 'waymarking' was not even thought of. The only other maps available to walkers were the Ordnance Survey one-inch which showed many paths, but the scale was too small and it was left to the rambler to find his way from one stile to another, whereas the six-inch maps showed the footpath clearly in relation to the hedges and the size of the fields, much as the post-war 1:25000 maps do today. And so, armed with his maps, the leader would pioneer his ramble certain that when leading his party of perhaps fifteen to twenty-five ramblers he was on the right track and was not likely to be challenged with trespassing. He was able to open up little-known paths which were definitely rights of way but not readily discernible, although the presence of stiles proved the existence of the paths.

In its early days the Club rambled only on Saturday afternoons as it was the general practice to work on Saturday mornings. It was important therefore that there should be somewhere to stop for tea in the early evening so that the walk should be of a reasonable distance, and if suggestions for a new ramble were offered to the Committee a tea-place had to be recommended at the same time. In the short days of the late Autumn, the Winter and the early Spring we would finish the walk in the dark, but there was very little traffic in the lanes and it was safe to make our way homeward, keeping together and using torches where necessary. Rambles usually started from local stations and most of these are still open, although the line from Redditch to Alcester and beyond has been dismantled, and stations on the Nuneaton line at Coleshill and Arley and Fillongley have been closed for some time.

Dress and footwear was something we took seriously. We did not have the advantage of modern anoraks and had to manage very often with cycling capes and sou'westers. Our footwear, both for ladies and gents, would be strong boots into which we ourselves had hammered hob nails. It is important to be dry and have comfortable boots (or shoes) if you want to enjoy a day in the country.

The boundaries of Birmingham have been extended quite a lot since I first joined the Club, so that some of the walks which were popular with Club members before the 1939-1945 War (e.g. from Yardley church, through Marston Green and Chelmsley Woods to Coleshill) are no longer country walks. As the boundaries will inevitably extend further still as time marches on, so we must enjoy our local rambles while we can.

'Let this book be your guide'.

A rambling group from Birmingham C.H.A. on the River Alne near Tanworth in Arden on February 24th. 1912.

Foreword

OUR BOOK contains twenty-two walks listed in a clockwise direction around the West Midlands, commencing and finishing at Tanworth in Arden, where members of the Birmingham C.H.A. have assisted the Parish Council with footpath work over the past two years.

All the footpaths in the area have been cleared and refurbished, which included the replacing of over 100 stiles and a number of sleeper bridges, footbridges and kissing gates. 550 waymark arrows were used.

All the walks can be undertaken from central Birmingham using public transport. Up-to-date times etc. can be obtained by telephoning the Centro Hotline: 021 200 2700.

We would like to thank everyone who has contributed to the book in any way, and we hope that it will be a source of pleasure for all country-lovers.

Tom Birch

Mary Wall

Abbreviations used in the text and the maps

B.S.	Bus stop
C.H.A.	Countrywide Holidays Association
F.B.	Footbridge
G.R.	Grid reference
H.O.E.W.	Heart of England Way
M.R.N.	Midland Red North
M.R.S.	Midland Red South
M.R.W.	Midland Red West
N.T.	National Trust
N.W.P.	North Worcestershire Path
O.S.	Ordnance Survey
P	Parking
P.H.	Public House
Sch	School
Sta	Station
W.M.T.	West Midlands Transport

Another photograph from the archives. Claverdon, October 1911.

Publishers' Note

Every care has been taken in the preparation of this book. All the walks have been independently checked and are believed to be correct at the time of publication. However, neither the Birmingham C.H.A. Rambling Club nor the publishers can accept responsibility for any errors or omissions or for any loss, damage, injury or inconvenience resulting from the use of the book.

Please remember that the countryside is continually changing: hedges and fences may be removed or re-sited; landmarks may disappear; footpaths may be re-routed or be ploughed over and not reinstated (as the law requires); concessionary paths may be closed. The publishers would be very pleased to have details of any such changes that are observed by readers.

Location Map

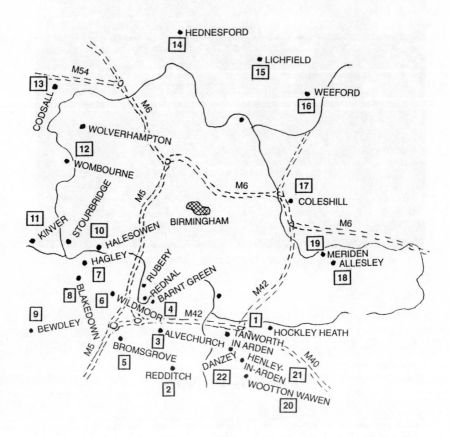

HEDNESFORD

14

LICHFIELD

15

WEEFORD

16

M54

13

CODSALL

M6

WOLVERHAMPTON

12

WOMBOURNE

M6

COLESHILL

17

STOURBRIDGE

M5

M6

11

KINVER

10

HALESOWEN

BIRMINGHAM

19

MERIDEN

ALLESLEY

18

HAGLEY

7

RUBERY

REDNAL

BARNT GREEN

M42

8

BLAKEDOWN

6

WILDMOOR

4

M42

HOCKLEY HEATH

1

9

BEWDLEY

M5

TANWORTH
IN ARDEN

3

ALVECHURCH

BROMSGROVE

HENLEY-
IN-ARDEN

M40

5

DANZEY

21

REDDITCH

22

2

WOOTTON WAWEN

20

Tanworth-in-Arden

by John Benbow

Maps: Landranger 139; Pathfinder 954
Start: Earlswood Station (G.R. 095743)
Finish: Hockley Heath (G.R. 152730) or Dorridge (G.R. 170749)
Length of ramble: 10 miles or (shorter route finishing at Hockley Heath)
8 miles
Transport: Train from Birmingham Snow Hill to Earlswood (outward
journey). Train from Dorridge to Birmingham (return), or X20 Stratford
Blue Bus from Hockley Heath (return)
Terrain: Fairly flat and easy; may be muddy near lake at Earlswood
Refreshments: P.H. at Tanworth-in-Arden and Hockley Heath

O N ARRIVAL at Earlswood Station, turn left through the car park and along Station Drive. Turn right into Rumbush Lane and after 50 yds turn right again over a stile onto a hedged path, then straight ahead over an open field to another stile into Clowes Wood.

Turn right to follow the edge of the wood, bearing left near a railway footbridge, to continue along the main track. This runs alongside the railway for approx. 200 yds, before gradually veering away. Continue for another 500 yds to where a distinct path goes off on the right over a plank bridge. Follow along this path for some distance, crossing two more plank bridges, in quick succession, keeping to the right-hand track at all times.

On reaching a footbridge turn right onto a track, with Terry's pool on the left and a deep ditch on the right. After about 150 yds the path veers right to a stile. From here, turn immediately left along a wide grassy track and through a gate into Clowes Wood Lane at Rose Farm. Continue along the lane to a T-junction, then turn right into Malthouse Lane to cross over the railway with Terrys Green Farm on the right. Continue to the next road junction.

When the road swings right carry straight on past the 'No Through Road' sign and a large residence 'Rose Common', on the right, until the M42 is reached. Turn left here, alongside the motorway on a track, dropping down to the railway. Pass under the M42, with the railway on left, to enter a field. Cross this diagonally to a corner stile, then with a hedge and ditch on the left, continue to a second stile and into Wood Lane. Turn left along the lane to the Royal Oak Pub. Cross the main road to take a footpath opposite the P.H., which leads through a copse and over a stile into a field, then continue with a hedge on the left.

Bear diagonally right in the second field to reach a level crossing. Go over the railway lines, turn left along a hedge in the next field, then take

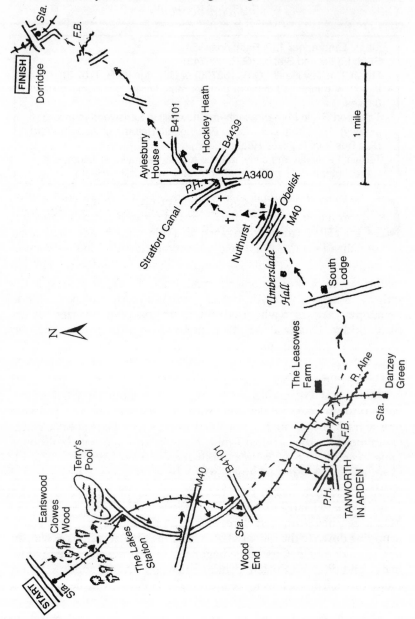

a bearing right to a footbridge over the River Alne. With a hedge now on the right follow through two fields to a stile in the top corner and then with a fence on the right to a lane. Turn left here to enter the picturesque village of Tanworth-in-Arden.

Crossing the Green to the church, leave the village through a gate at the top of stone steps into the churchyard, stopping to admire the open views across South Warwickshire as the path drops down to an iron gate into a lane (The Butts). Turn right here, then after about 30 yds take a footpath on the left, soon crossing a stile, keeping a hedge on the right in the first field, then on the left in the next field. A sharp right-hand turn along the hedge leads to a footbridge over the River Alne.

Head diagonally right to a tunnel under the railway and take a signposted path veering right to a stile at the edge of a copse. Walk straight across the field, passing a large oak tree in the centre, to reach a marker post in the far hedge. Turn left here along the hedge to a gate. Continue for a few yards on the same heading to the second gap on the right to go through another gate (waymarked) and over a stream. Turn left immediately and proceed, keeping a hedge on the left, through three fields until a crossroads of paths is reached.

Turn left here and continue with a hedge now on the right, crossing a stile over a ditch into a plantation to another stile and ditch. The path now veers gradually right following the hedge line to the lane at South Lodge at Umberslade Hall.

Turn left and continue for approx. 300 yds to take a marked path alongside the edge of the estate, with the Hall on the left. Keeping to the left-hand fence, pass through open parkland (with its beautiful old trees). When a marker post is reached, bear right, through an iron gate, into a field to head for a stile and bridge under M42.

Turn right along the lane, then left on a path, just before a cottage, to a stile leading into a field. The path goes diagonally across the first field, then with a hedge on the right in a second field to reach Umberslade Baptist Church. From the corner left of the church, take the tarmac drive down to the road, turning right here to the main Stratford Road at Hockley Heath. (The X20 bus may be caught here to return to Birmingham).

To continue the longer ramble, turn left on reaching the main Stratford Road, cross and then turn right onto Aylesbury Road, by the Nags Head Pub. At a sharp bend in the road go left through a white gate on a grassy track, crossing the drive to Aylesbury House Hotel. Go straight ahead through a wooden gate to a stile, keeping a hedge on the left in the next two fields, until a marker post is seen on the left.

The path swings here to a stile onto a lane. Turn left and continue for about 50 yds, then take the path on the right along a rough stony track until a hedge is reached. Turn left along the near side of the hedge, crossing two stiles, and, keeping the hedge on the right, continue on a grassy track to a lane (passing a barn on the left). Go straight ahead here over a stile to cross a large field to a footbridge over a brook and a stile into parkland. Cross to a narrow lane, bearing slightly left from the brook. In this lane is the house where Edith Holden lived – the author of the *Diary of an Edwardian Country Lady*. This lane leads into Arden Lane, then down to the main road at Dorridge. Turn right here for the railway station.

In Tanworth-in-Arden

Walk 2
Old Yarr
by Margot Baggott

Maps: Landranger 150; Pathfinder 975
Start & Finish: Redditch (G.R. 038676)
Length of ramble: 8½ miles.
Shorter alternative: 6 miles* (see footnote)
Transport: Train from New Street to Redditch or Bus (M.R.W. 146 from Birmingham Bus Station to Redditch Kingfisher Centre).
Car Park in Morton Stanley Park (G.R. 030652)
Special features: 'Old Yarr' in picturesque setting, and panoramic views from ridge near Hunt End.
Refreshments: Redditch and P.H. at Hunt End

L EAVE Redditch railway station by turning right out of the car park onto Bromsgrove Road. After about 300 yds there is a pathway on the left running alongside Holmwood Drive, opposite a football club. Take this path, known as Muskett's Way, passing Pitcher Oak Wood on the right and a golf course on the left. Carry on across a high footbridge over the A448 and continue on path to a minor road.

Cross over, then turn right and continue for approx. 20 yds, then left down another walkway opposite Woodend Close, passing under a road bridge and then branching left at a T-junction of paths. Exercise bars are soon in evidence on the left of the path and the entrance to the golf club after a short distance on the right. Continue on the same heading until the path runs alongside Windmill Drive, after which an entrance into Morton Stanley Park is soon reached. *(See footnote)**

Cross the park diagonally, keeping left until a small pool is reached and look for a break in the hedge. Walk straight towards a grassy bank, taking a broad green track to the right of a stile. This leads up through the trees to a stile and out to a housing development. Go over the road, turn right and continue for a few yards then bear left and keep to footpath leading into Woodgreen Close. Then take a path on the left

* *The ramble could be shortened by using own transport to start and finish at the car park in Morton Stanley Park, off Windmill Drive.*

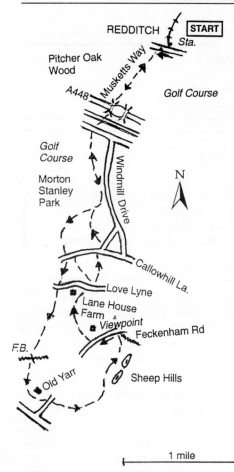

between houses and turn right on reaching the road. Proceed to the T-junction, then left into Callow Hill Lane.

Cross the road and turn right, passing cottages and a bridle path on the left, then take a gate on the left a little further on. Go across the middle of a rough pasture, leaving bushes and scrub on the left, until near the end of the field. Here descend a steep bank which drops down to a stile opposite Lane House Farm — a beautiful half-timbered farmhouse.

Turn right up the lane (Love Lyne) and take a signposted path over a stile which is on the left after a short distance. Follow the left-hand hedge through fields and over several stiles, until an enclosed area known as Fox Covert is reached in the left-hand corner of the field. Just to the right of this is a wooden footbridge. Cross this and also a metal bridge over a fishing lake. There is also a wire fence to be climbed here. Turn left on a track and continue on the same heading (S.W.) passing through a gate, then make a beeline for the edge of a wooded area at the top of the field. Over the fence an abundance of primroses can be seen in Spring. Continue along the edge of the wood to a stile in the bottom corner. In the next field a few yards on is a footbridge on the left, leading to a neatly cut archway in the hedge. This leads to the garden of 'Old Yarr', a beautiful house which was once a mill. A right of way goes along a paved path, past the front door of the house and down the drive, turning left over a stile onto Blaze Lane.

Opposite is a signpost and gate into a field. Cross diagonally left, and pass through a gate at the far side, then follow the stream on the right for approx. 25 yds to a footbridge hidden in the hedge. Keeping in line with the bridge go up the field to the top left-hand corner, aiming for a cluster of trees. Go through the large, metal gate on the left and cross the field to a gate on the left of Astwood Hall Farm buildings into the next field. Cross this field, passing farm outbuildings on the right, then make for two gates and go through the left-hand one.

Continue straight on, past an old wind pump to a stile and keeping a hedge on the left pass a gate on the left and follow the stream through fields for about a quarter of a mile, until a small arched bridge and stile is reached in the far corner. This leads to a path between hedges to a lane at Hunt End. Turn left down Feckenham Road, past Mill Cottages which were old needle mills. (Other examples of mills are to be found dotted all around Redditch wherever there is a convenient source of water.) A mill pond used to be on the opposite side of the road.

After a few yards, take a waymarked drive on the right. Go up the driveway towards the house and turn left to a stile near the teak gates, (a Union Jack is usually fluttering here). Glance over the hedge to admire the beautifully manicured gardens. T he raised seat is for the owners of the house to see over the hedge and across the valley with its magnificent panorama. To the left is the Ridgeway, straight ahead the Severn Valley, whilst Bredon Hill and the Malverns can be seen a little

Old Yarr (sketched by Michael Baggott)

further to the right. Feckenham Church Tower is visible in the middle distance.

Follow the hedge on the right, along the top of the bank, disregarding a stile on the right, until a stile is reached at the end of the ridge. Climb this and proceed straight down the bank to another stile, leading back out onto Love Lyne at Lane House Farm. Turn right and take a bridleway on the left a short way along. (*See footnote*)* On a bend in the track there is a stile on the right, go over this and follow the path round the hill to the exit gates and stile on Callow Hill Lane.

Turn right and continue for a few yards and then go left up Morton Lane to a stile on the left into Walkwood Coppice. Take the right-hand path through wood and down to stile leading into Morton Stanley Park. Proceed to the top end of the park, past the play area and out onto Windmill Drive. Turn left and follow the same route back as on the outward journey.

Don't forget to make a right turn just past the exercise bars and a right turn on reaching the road. After approx. 20 yds a path on the left leads to the footbridge over the A448 and along Muskett's Way back onto the Bromsgrove Road. Turn right to the rail and bus stations.

---

*   *After rain a less muddy alternative would be to go through the gate on the left of the bridle path, climbing uphill to a gate in Callow Hill Lane, then turning right for about 300 yds to reach Morton Lane.*

Rowney Green and Hob Hill

by Barbara and Howard Penn

Maps: Landranger 139; Pathfinder 954
Start & Finish: Alvechurch (GR 022720)
Length of ramble: 8 miles
Transport from Birmingham: Train from New St. Station to Alvechurch
Parking: Car Park in Alvechurch (half a mile from station)
Terrain: Undulating – two short but moderate hill climbs
Points of interest: Good open views from Newbourne Hill and Hob Hill
Refreshments: Red Lion Inn and shops in Alvechurch

COMMENCE at Alvechurch Station by turning right on leaving the platform to walk parallel with the track for 100 yds, before taking a path on the left through a gap in the hedge. This leads into Station Road. Turn right here, then take a right-hand fork into School Lane, bearing right again and following downhill to the main Redditch Road (A441).

Cross and turn right, then after a few yards turn left along a bridleway heading east, downhill initially, to go under the bypass. Almost immediately climb a stile on the right onto a field path which rises gradually, passing through a small gate and crossing a footbridge over a stream. Go straight ahead through fields and over two further stiles, before reaching the trees on Newbourne Hill. Pause here to look back at the splendid view, which includes the Lickey Hills in the middle distance and Frankley Beeches to the right on the sky line.

Enter Newbourne Wood through a gap in the trees and up a flight of steps, to follow alongside a fenced off section of a nature reserve. The path turns right to follow the paddock fence and emerges on the main road at Rowney Green. Turn left here, then first right into Chapel Lane, to walk downhill. When the road turns right keep straight on along a wide farm track and when this ends follow in the same direction through stables and downhill on a field path to pass a small pool at the bottom. Cross a stream, then bear left immediately to climb a stile into another field. Keeping to the right-hand hedge and to the left of the stream, follow through several fields, turning right over the second footbridge to reach a lane at Lillicot Farm.

A surfaced footpath opposite leads through more fields and crosses a farm track, before reaching a road to the left of a converted house

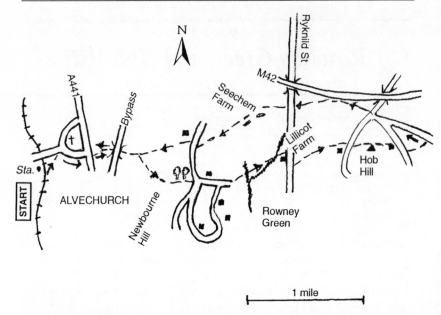

called 'Chimneys'. Cross straight over to climb Hob Hill, bearing diagonally left to the trig point. This is a good spot for a picnic lunch and offers an excellent panorama.

From the trig point go straight ahead to climb a stile, cross a field and another stile, then keeping Hob Hill Farm on the left, climb a third stile onto a road. Turn right here and continue for a short distance, passing a track on the right to 'Windy Ridge'. Just beyond this turn left through a gate to follow a footpath along the left-hand edge of fields and a line of oak trees. After approx. 400 yds go over a waymarked stile on the left. Keep forward along the wire fence, bearing left onto a bridle track. Continue straight ahead on reaching the road, passing Billesley Farm to a T-junction.

Cross straight over to take a 'No Through Road' then go through wooden gates and past farm buildings. Follow the bridleway back to Rowney Green, passing alongside the M42 to a road junction near a bridge. Turn left and then right almost immediately to take another bridleway, leading to Seechem Farm. Here fork right along a fenced path to meet a surfaced track, then turn left and keep straight ahead to pass through two farm gates close together and into a field (Equestrian Centre nearby).

Continue in a south west direction on a wide farm track, passing through several good farm gates, until the path emerges onto a road at

Rowney Green House Farm. Turn right here and after a short distance go left onto a bridleway leading back to Alvechurch to join up with the outward route near the new bypass. On reaching the Redditch Road cross over with care, turning right for a few yards, then left into School Lane. This winds upwards to pass near to the church, bearing left into Station Road and left again to reach the drive to Alvechurch Station for the train back to Birmingham.

Walk 4
Cattespool
by Tom Webster

Maps: Landranger 139; Pathfinder 953 and 954
Length of ramble: 10 miles, 8 miles or 7 miles (See footnote*)
Start: Rednal (G.R. 999764) or Barnt Green (G.R. 006737)
Finish: Rednal (G.R. 999764) or Alvechurch (G.R. 022720)
Transport from Birmingham: W.M.T. 62 bus to Rednal (terminus) and
return. Train New Street to Barnt Green. From Alvechurch by train or
M.R.W. 146 bus
Parking: Car park at Rednal – adjacent to Visitors' Centre
Terrain: Easy. One steep climb can be avoided near beginning,
otherwise changes in height are gradual
Special features: Open views, good for bird-watching alongside Bittell
Reservoir; and Cofton Hackett church is worth a visit
Refreshments: Hare and Hounds Pub. and Visitors' Centre at Rednal,
Lickey Visitors' Centre on Bilberry Hill, Crown Inn at Withybed Green
and Red Lion at Alvechurch.

FROM the terminus of the W.M.T. 62 bus at Rednal walk straight ahead, passing the Hare and Hounds on the right and the Visitors' Centre and car park on the left. Cross at the lights and proceed to the traffic island, turning right past Bilberry Hill Training Centre. After 200 yds take the second of two bridges on the left to cross a ditch and a stream.

Immediately over the stream take the steps on the left to climb steeply onto Bilberry Hill. (This can be avoided, by going straight ahead on the lower track to the Visitors' Centre). At the top of the steps turn left and when the track levels out it is worth pausing to admire the view to the right. Continue for approx. 100 yds on the main track before

---

* *The walk may be shortened by approximately two miles either by starting the ramble from Barnt Green railway station (❀ on page 14) or by continuing straight along the lane at Withybed Green (✿ on page 14), passing the Crown pub. and over the canal bridge to follow the road into Alvechurch. The bus route (M.R.W. 146) is on the main road in Alvechurch and the railway station is to the south of the village.*

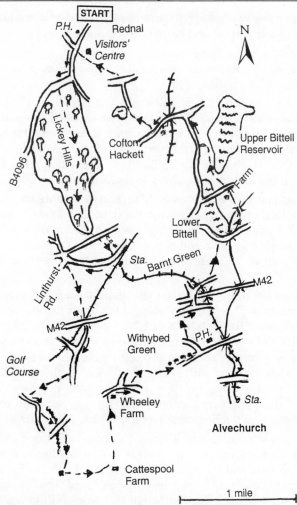

taking the right-hand fork (views now to the left). Almost immediately fork right again on a grassy track and proceed due south until a wide track goes off on the right. This leads downhill to the Visitors' Centre.

From the Centre walk straight across the grass to pick up a main path leading downhill through trees on the left of the valley, which passes a wooden shelter on the left after about half a mile. Shortly after this the path swings right over a stream, then after approx. 400 yds passes another shelter on the right. The woods at this point are especially attractive in late spring at bluebell time. Continue on the main track until it emerges on a road opposite Cherry Hill House, where turn left for a few yards and cross to steps leading onto a tree-lined path through to another road and Barnt Green Station. Here turn right.

❀ *Starting point for shorter walk*
On arriving by train from Birmingham, cross over the bridge and turn left out of the railway station.

Proceed for approximately half a mile to a T-junction, then turn left into Linthurst Road. After 50 yds take a waymarked footpath on the left, passing through several gates to reach a stile into a field. With a hedge on the left continue to the next stile, then bear half left in the next field to a stile near a large house. The path goes along a fence to pass left of the house and over a railway to reach a road.

Turn right under the motorway (M42) and walk straight ahead along Blackwell Road to a road junction on the right. Continue straight on for a further 300 yds to a stile on the right and proceed at right angles on a well defined path across a golf course. On reaching a 'green' just before a pool the path veers right to a gate leading onto a drive near the Club House.

Here turn left to the road, then left again to reach a stile on the left as the road bends. This path runs alongside a brook to the next stile and out onto the road. Turn left for about 75 yds before taking a signposted stile on the right. With a hedge on the right in the next two fields continue past a cottage and then through a gate into the adjacent field. Turn sharp left to follow with a hedge on the left, ignoring the first gate. Continue uphill and through a second gate onto a bridleway which leads to Cattespool Farm. After going through another gate pass between buildings (arched) and over a stile onto a broad track.

Here turn left and proceed along the ridge, with open views on either side and in front. The track ends at Wheeley Farm, where turn right on the road and keep straight ahead, passing Wheeley Road on the left. Just beyond the last of three cottages, called 'The Cottage' climb a stile on the left. Keeping the hedge and fence on the right follow through fields and over several stiles to reach Foxhill Lane.

Cross over to take the footpath opposite, alongside a high wall, signposted to Withybed Green. Follow the waymarkers downhill through fields to reach a row of cottages. (The Crown pub. is about 100 yds further on).

✿ *See footnote on page 12 for the shorter alternative route from this point.*

To continue on the main walk, after passing cottages turn left into Birches Lane and follow this until it peters out, then take the bridlepath to Coopers Hill. On reaching the road turn right, then first left over the motorway (M42) and right into Aqueduct Lane. After crossing over the railway continue for 150 yds to the 'Paddocks' on the left, from where the footpath leads along a tarmac drive. Where the drive veers left go straight ahead over the grass to a waymarked path between trees, leading into a field. Bear diagonally left to a stile, then with a hedge on the right follow downhill to a road (good open views to the left here).

Turn right on the road, passing over the canal and proceed to the bend in the road where a footpath on the left is signposted 'Upper Bittell Reservoir'. Take this, and after crossing a brook, go diagonally right across a large field to a stile leading onto the canal bridge. From here the track goes to Bittell Farm, veering right, then left around buildings to a lane.

Cross to a footpath opposite and follow along a green track between a fence and hedge, with good views over to the Lickey Hills on the left. The path passes a deep hollow, (disused pit), before reaching a stile, then with a fence on the right bear slightly downhill to a further stile. From here the path goes along the embankment of the picturesque Upper Bittell Reservoir, which belongs to the British Waterways Board and feeds the Worcestershire & Birmingham Canal. At the end of the dam the path turns left to pass the remains of an old stone pump house and out onto a bridleway.

Here turn right alongside a pool, then left at a T-junction and continue along a lane to pass under the railway and then by Cofton Hackett church on the left. This was built in the nineteenth century and has some interesting features, including a pinnacled bellcote. A little further along the lane, opposite a large house on the left, a stile on the right leads onto a field path. Climb this and proceed with a hedge on the right, then when the hedge ends the path strikes uphill to reach a surfaced track. Turn right and continue over the dam and through gate to reach Chestnut Drive, then ahead to a T-junction at Groveley Lane.

Cross over with care, bearing left onto a track through the trees, then diagonally right across Cofton Park, heading to the left of a line of four trees, onto a tarmac path. This leads to the main road at Rednal, near the Visitors' Centre. The W.M.T. 62 bus stop for returning to Birmingham is a little further to the left on the opposite side.

Dodford

by Sam and June Cordwell

Maps: Landranger 139; Pathfinder 953
Start & Finish: Lower Sidemoor (GR 954713)
Length of ramble: 7 miles
Transport from Birmingham: M.R.W. 143 to junction of Broad Street and Crabtree Lane, Lower Sidemoor, Nr. Bromsgrove
Parking: Crabtree Lane
Terrain: Undulating: Hilly in places: Woodland paths
Special feature: Woodland and meadow flowers in early spring and summer
Refreshments: Inn and shops at Sidemoor

FROM the bus stop at Lower Sidemoor, near the lower end of Broad Street, walk towards 'Pleck Stores' at the T-junction and turn right into Crabtree Lane. Cross over and continue along the lane as far as Parkwood Road. Turn left here, then right into Lynden Close and at the end of the cul-de-sac go through a wooden gate on the right into a field. Follow the path on the left hand side to Perryfields Road, cross over and go through a tall kissing gate a few yards to the right, then along a surfaced drive.

After about 100 yds take a hedged path slightly to the left between orchards, leading to a footbridge over the M5 motorway. On the far side climb a stile to follow a path which bears right to cross a stream into a field. Continue straight ahead to a fence/stile in the opposite hedge, then keep on the same heading to go uphill to reach the tree line and continue to another stile, with a farm on the right. Bear half right downhill to a stile in the corner of a field leading to a lane.

Take the stile opposite, then bear slightly left uphill across this field to another stile, then straight ahead to a double stile. Go straight ahead in the next field to enter a wooded area, then down a steep slope to a footbridge at the bottom. Turn left and follow a field path over two more stiles, before turning left again onto a surfaced bridle track to reach a lane. Cross to the stile, almost opposite, to follow along a wire fence on the field path which rises gradually to a stile ahead. From here a hedged path leads onto a metalled road with a large house on left.

Continue to where the lane bends right and climb the stile ahead into a field. The path slopes down to a little wooden footbridge, leading

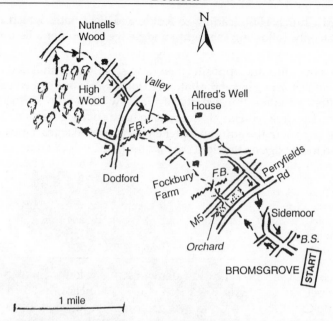

over a stile into High Wood. Bear right to follow a waymarked path uphill through the wood, ignoring cross tracks, and continue until the path bears a little to the right. Follow this up to the top, from where it winds gently downhill, with a wire fence on the left.

Turn left at the bottom to climb a stile, then right along a track past Highwood Cottage and through a gate onto a fenced path. At the far end another gate leads to a winding track through Nutnells Wood, attractive especially in autumn, although inclined to be muddy. A gate at the far end leads into a lane.

Turn right, then immediately right again to climb a stile, then across a paddock and over another stile to enter more woodland. Continue for a short distance, before climbing a stile into a field. Keeping the hedge on the left, continue to another stile, then turn right and with a hedge on the right go up a grassy slope, passing a small pool on the right. Straight ahead is a railing stile; go over this to follow the edge of the next field, with the wood on the right and trees on the left. The path bears left to reach a wooden bridge over a stream. Cross this and climb steps up a slope to follow a narrow path, which passes between two houses to emerge on a road.

Turn left, then right after a few yards into Church Road, and admire good distant views, before dropping down to the bottom of the hill, past crossroads. Take a waymarked track opposite which goes to the left of

Dodford Church Hall, leading to a stile and field path, which rises uphill steeply, following the right hand hedge to another stile onto a lane.

Cross over the stile opposite, then drop steeply downhill and over another stile, turning left at the bottom to follow a pleasant green valley. This offers an interesting variety of meadow flowers in spring and summer. The dreaded Himalayan balsam has also made its home here, and can be seen in the autumn. After crossing several stiles, ignoring a stile and footbridge on the right *en route*, the path leads out onto a road.

A scene near High Close Wood, Dodford

Turn right, leaving Nibbletts Hill on the left, and continue on the road past Alfred's Well House at which point the road bends to the right and climbs quite steeply. Where it forks at the top of the hill, bear left. After a few yards turn right through a field gate then, keeping a hedge on the left, continue to a gap in the hedge now on the right. Cross two stiles at the bottom, then strike uphill on a field path to a stile in the corner, to the right of Fockbury Farm buildings. Follow over one more field to a lane, from where there is a good distant view of the Catshill area.

Turn right along the lane, crossing a bridge over the M5 and continue to a T-junction, before turning right into Perryfields Road. Cross over into a lane, passing market gardens on the left and houses on the right. Ignore the path on the left and go forward through a gate onto a well defined path leading back into Crabtree Lane. Continue straight down, turning left at the bottom into Broad Street, for the bus back to Birmingham. (No sign, but wait opposite the one used on the outward journey).

Nutnells Wood

Walk 6
Wildmoor
by Madge Smith

Maps: Landranger 139; Pathfinder 953
Start: Rednal (G.R. 999764)
Finish: Gannow (G.R. 990773)
Length of ramble: 8 miles
Transport: W.M.T. 62 bus outward to Birmingham boundary at Rednal,
W.M.T. 61 bus return from Gannow to City centre
Refreshments: Pubs. at Rednal and Wildmoor; Visitors' Centres at
Rednal and Waseley
Features: Open views from Beacon Hill and Waseley Hills
Terrain: Undulating – several short climbs

FROM the terminus of the W.M.T. 62 bus at Rednal, pass the Visitors' Centre on the left and cross at the traffic lights. Follow the sign to the 'Lickey Hills Nature Reserve', bearing right with the road, to reach the Old Rose and Crown hotel. Here turn right to pass in front of the hotel, then left through the car park, to a path between the golf shop and the course. This rises gradually to a flight of steps, goes over a cross track and up more steps, before reaching a well defined track on the tree line.

Turn right, then left after a few yards and at the top of the slope bear right. Continue straight ahead on the main track, keeping a pinewood copse on the left, to take a narrow path through the trees leading to the trig point on Beacon Hill (987'). Veer left past the trig point to follow the path along a grassy ridge from where there is a good distant view of the City and of Frankley Beeches in the middle distance.

On reaching a marker post (N.W.P.) on the ridge, turn 90° left and make straight across the hill. Notice a 'fortified' toposcope about 20 yds to the left and proceed on the same heading, with the pinewood copse still on the left, to go through a gap in the far hedge onto a track. Turn right here and follow the track, keeping to the right-hand fence, to reach Monument Road. Cross over and turn left for a few yards before taking a footpath sign on the right to 'Beacon Lane and Bristol Road'. This leads across a field and over a drive to a stile, then across two more fields, rising uphill to reach Beacon Lane.

Turn left down the lane for 150 yds to Beacon Farm, then right on a track to enter Beacon Wood, noted for its bluebells in Spring. Continue

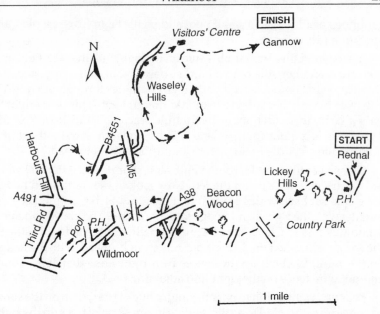

on the main track to pass a stone seat on the right of the path, laid in memory of Alderman Jack Wood. Shortly after this, look for a pedestrian path on the left, which runs alongside the main bridlepath and avoids mud after heavy rain. At the bottom a gate leads onto a surfaced track, passing through a landscaped garden and Winsel Cottage (N.T.).

The track continues to emerge on a lane, where turn left and then right almost immediately to pass under a road bridge (A38). Proceed along Redhill Lane, passing Chadwich Manor on the right – a nineteenth century mansion (N.T.). On reaching a sign to Manor Farm, turn left and just beyond farm buildings go through the left-hand gate onto a narrow track. After approx. 50 yds climb a stile in the left-hand hedge which leads to a small plantation. The path follows along a wire fence on the left to a stile and into an open field. Go straight ahead here, bearing right after about 50 yds to go through a tunnel under the M5 Motorway.

On leaving the tunnel, bear left into a field, then sharp right to follow a hedge to a stile in the far corner and out onto a main road. Cross to Wildmoor Lane opposite and continue along here to take the first turning on the right. Cross a piece of rough ground on the left, used as an extra car park for the Wildmoor P.H. nearby. Climb a stile, then walk diagonally right across the field to a stile immediately on the right and continue ahead to pass a small pool and picnic table. This is a pleasant spot for a picnic lunch.

Just beyond this area climb a stile on the right into the next field and then cross another stile onto a hard surface. From a stile opposite, the way leads first onto a fenced path, then continues through open fields and over two further stiles to rejoin Wildmoor Lane. This bears right to pass a farm, then after about half a mile reaches 'Third Road' on the right. This is a quiet country lane which winds for about a third of a mile, passing Middle Road, before joining a busy main road.

Cross over to go up Harbours Hill, almost opposite. After 500 yds a red quarry cliff appears on the left. Now look in the right-hand hedge for a stile set back which leads into a meadow. Strike uphill, keeping parallel with the right-hand hedge to a stile ahead. The view is opening up now, across to Clent. Here bear diagonally right to a double stile in the corner of the next field, then continue straight ahead, with the hedge on the right, to climb a wire fence. Turn right immediately to climb another wire fence on the right into adjoining field.

Bear half right uphill to pass through a line of trees, then on the same bearing drop downhill to a stile. Follow down a line of trees on the right to another stile, then straight ahead to an exit stile, left of a farm, onto the road. Turn left here and cross over to take the first right into Malthouse Lane, then fork left under the motorway bridge. Bear left at a T-junction and after 20 yds look for a stile in the right-hand hedge. This leads up the edge of a long field to a stile in the top corner. Over this a cross track offers a choice of ways: *the higher route is recommended for views The lower route is inclined to be muddy. For the higher route continue from the next paragraph; for the lower route continue from ❀ below.*

Higher route: Turn right for 25 yds, before turning left through a metal gate, to the left of a stile, and into a field. The way leads uphill steadily, following the left-hand hedge, pausing *en route* to admire the view. At the top go through a wooden gate into a small plantation and continue straight ahead on a bridle path to reach a kissing gate, turning left onto the open hillside. Strike uphill to the highest point on the ridge and from here straight on towards the trig point, following a waymark to keep a wire fence on the left. The views are excellent and well worth the initial climb. Soon after passing the trig point the path drops downhill to Waseley Visitors' Centre. (*Now continue from the final paragraph.*)

❀ *Lower route*: Turn left on the cross track to contour Windmill Hill, passing through a gate *en route* and continue until the track emerges on a lane near the farm. Ignore a left turn and follow along the lane past houses. Soon after the last house a path slants off to the right and leads to a stile. The way then follows the edge of fields to climb two stiles close together. From here the Waseley Centre can be seen on the left near the bottom of the next field.

From the Centre a surfaced track goes between the car park and play area. When this ends, turn left onto a broad green track, along a fenced way, to reach the road at Gannow. Cross over into Boleyn Road opposite for the W.M.T.61 bus back to Birmingham or W.M.T. 49 to Solihull.

'Ramparts' on Beacon Hill

Harborough Hill
by Peggy Armstrong

O.S. Maps: Landranger 139; Pathfinder 933 and 953
Start & Finish: West Hagley (G.R. 901805)
Length of Ramble: 9 Miles. Shorter Route (*see *footnote on page 26*):
7 miles
Transport from Birmingham: Train from New St. to Hagley (Return)
Terrain: Hilly in places. Easy field paths from Broome to Clent
Parking: Lane adjacent to Hagley Station (Access from A456 and M5)
Refreshments: Hill Tavern, Clent (slight diversion from main track)

TURN left on leaving the station platform to climb the steps into Station Road, turning left over the railway and continuing into Brake Lane. After half a mile take the footpath on the left at 'Chimneys' where the path runs between hedges, passing through a gate into a field. With the hedge now on the left and Brakemill plantation to the right of farmland continue to a meeting of paths. Cross straight over to pass a cottage on the right and follow a tarmac track, passing another residence on the left and private woodland to the right. To the left can also be seen a restored mill and stream.

After about 200 yds a stile leads to a fenced path, with meadows on the right and after a further 50 yds a glance to the left through bushes gives a view of one of a number of small pools in the area, ablaze with water lilies in July.

A stile to the end of this track leads into Stakenbridge Lane with a farm on the right. Cross the lane and turn left to walk under a railway bridge. From this point take the first of two paths signposted to 'Blakedown' and, ignoring the tarmac drive to the right, continue on a track passing Randon Cottage. A little further on pass through a gate into a field with Harborough Hill on the left. Keeping a hedge on the right go through another gate and after 15 yds look for a signpost which stands at the junction of a bridlepath and footpaths. Turn left here in the direction of the arrow and continue to the corner of the field. Again turn left, continue for a few yards, cross the main road with care and take the footpath opposite. Cross the field diagonally left to go through trees, passing a pond on the right to reach an open field and a marker post. Turn right, then left after a few yards at another marker post, making towards woods.

At a cross track near the edge of the field, pass through a hedge gap onto a bridle track and strike uphill through trees on a well defined track. This gradually levels out, passing bushes and a ruined house on the right, then continues on field paths with a broken hedge on the left to the Stourbridge Road. Cross here, then turn left and continue for a few yards and take a signposted footpath over a stile, then go diagonally left to Broome Lane (Hundred Acres Farm on the right).

Turn right, then fork right after about 100 yds to pass Broome Church and Broome House to continue on the lane, passing 'Old Well' cottage with staddlestones in the garden. *Staddlestones were used as a foundation to support the corners of hayricks years ago.* Turn left on reaching the T-junction and follow a track bearing right, then left, and continue for about 200 yds., when the track merges into a field path. With a hedge on the left continue over stiles and several fields to a lane, with good views of Clent ahead.

On reaching the lane turn right and continue for 100 yds, then take the footpath on the left, climbing a steep bank to bear right into a field. Keep as near to the left hand hedge as possible. The path becomes more distinct and suddenly emerges into a 'green glade' (suitable lunch spot).

Continue along the pleasant grass track and through another field before dropping over a stile in the left-hand hedge into a high meadow

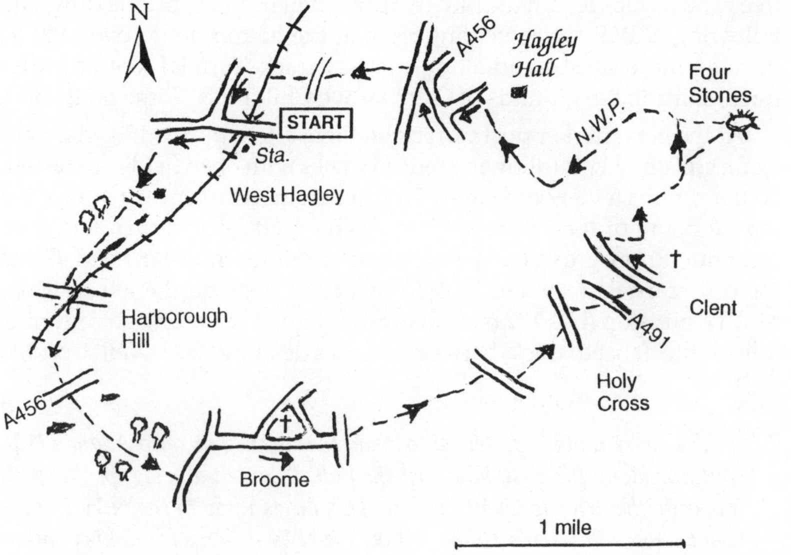

N

A456 Hagley Hall

Four Stones

START

N.W.P.

Sta.

West Hagley

Harborough Hill

Clent

A491

Holy Cross

A456

Broome

1 mile

with excellent views. Follow the right-hand hedge to a lane near Holy Cross. Cross over and turn left and continue for about 100 yds to a waymarked path opposite farm buildings. After climbing a stile into a field follow the right-hand hedge alongside a stream to cross a second stile, then bear slightly left, ignoring the footbridge on the right to an exit stile onto the Stourbridge Road.

Cross the dual carriageway with care and turn right, then after a few yards take a stile in the left-hand hedge (hidden by shrubs etc.). Cross the field diagonally right towards a black and white house and go over a stile into a lane. (Clent village and church can be visited by going a few hundred yards to the right).

 * *For a shorter route see footnote.*

Turn left and cross over to a footpath along a busy lane, with open views extending to the Malverns. After about 400 yds turn right and slightly backwards to cross a stile into meadow. Go straight ahead for 100 yds before striking left on a path uphill, then through bracken to another stile with a house on the left. Turn right here, then take the right fork to follow the main bridle track. The Hill Tavern lies in a hollow on the left. Continue along the ridge in a N.E. direction until the track veers right, then take a waymarked bridle path to the left. After approx. 500 yds turn left onto another waymarked path which winds down through trees and shrubs to join the N.W.P. Turn left here and continue downhill following N.W.P. signs, veering right at the bottom to go over a stile, through more shrubs and along a grassy track. Turn left onto a wider track, skirting the grounds of Clent Grove Children's Home on the left.

At the next marker post turn right, then, after approx. 150 yds, right again still on N.W.P. following fenced tracks with open fields on the left. To the right is a view of Hagley Hall, an eighteenth century house, the family home of the Littletons. On reaching Hall Lane, turn left, then right into Bromsgrove Lane which leads to Kidderminster Road. Cross the dual carriageway and look for a signed track on the left near the M.R.W. bus stop (bus 192 back to Birmingham if required). To continue, follow the fenced track between houses leading to a well trodden

---

 * *If the shorter route is preferred to avoid the steep climb onto Adam's Hill, continue along the busy lane past the pub. Turn left at a signposted path (opposite the drive to Clent House). This meets up with the N.W.P. near Clent Grove Children's Home. Follow the N.W.P. signs from this point as in the main text above.*

footpath through fields and over a series of stiles to Worcester Road. Cross here to take an enclosed path to a small housing estate. Wind down the road, veering right, until in the bottom right hand corner where a path leads over the railway and culvert to run along the right-hand edge of a school playing field. Climb the stile in the corner before turning left along a fenced path to a lane. A left turn here leads to a T-junction, where another left turn leads back to Hagley Station after 300 yds.

A view from the Clent Hills
Hereford & Worcester Countryside Service

Walk 8
The Vale of Churchill
by Ellen Clark.

Maps: Landranger 139; Pathfinder 953
Start and finish: Blakedown (G.R. 881787). Shorter route returning
from Hagley (G.R. 901805) – see page 29 (❀)
Length of ramble: 7½ miles or 5½ miles
Transport from Birmingham: Train from New Street to Blakedown.
Parking: In Blakedown village.
Terrain: Undulating, moderately hilly.
Special features: Picturesque village of Churchill and views from ridge
on Barnett Hill.
Refreshments: Inns and shops at Blakedown.

ON LEAVING the station platform at Blakedown, turn left, then right almost immediately along a track, passing bollards and continuing with houses on both sides, leading onto the main road (A456).

Turn left for 30 yds to a pelican crossing, then right along the main road, crossing Belbroughton Road. After passing the 'Old House at Home' continue for 400 yds before taking a track on the left opposite Churchill Lane. Go straight ahead for 100 yds, then take a bridle path on the right. The way is narrow and climbs steadily through trees to reach a lane.

Take a left turn here and continue along Sandy Lane to 'Hunter's Lodge', where the lane turns sharp right. Follow on the lane for another 50 yds, taking a sandy track on the left which climbs steadily. Continue along the ridge of Barnett Hill, admiring the views on either side, including the Malverns to the right and Clent Hills to the left. Approx. 300 yds after the path levels out, look for a stile on the left. This leads onto a narrow grass track, with a wire fence on the right. Near the bottom it passes a nursery on the right and finally joins a cross track.

Turn left for a few yards, then look for a gully on the right, just before the path opens out into a field. This goes through bushes and trees to a stile into a field, where footpath signs point along the right-hand hedge to pass through two metal gates before entering woodland. Here the path is narrow for about 250 yds, until a track from the left joins it and there is a wooden gate on the right. The path goes through this gate to enter a small wood and then out onto a well defined field path leading onto the B4188.

Cross straight over onto a bridle path, keeping woods on the right, until at the far end of a long field the path veers left to pass Broome Mill on the right. When the path joins the drive bear left to reach the A456. Cross with care, then turn right and continue for about 30 yds to a surfaced track, signposted on the left, which passes Harborough Farm. After a short distance the path becomes a green lane until it reaches a narrow road. Continue under the railway bridge to pass Stakenbridge Farm and a pool on the right.

❧ *Shorter route. If a shorter route is preferred, turn right over the stile at Stakenbridge Farm and continue, first with a pool on the right, then woods on the left to Brakemill Farm. Go straight on at a junction of paths for 25 yds, turning right onto a field path just beyond farm buildings. This is clearly marked and goes diagonally left to a stile and into Sweetpool Lane. Turn left here to a T-junction, then right and continue for about 300 yds to the railway station at Hagley.*

To complete the full walk, take a stile on the left about 100 yds after passing Stakenbridge Farm, into a field, noted for snowdrops in early Spring. The path continues through a gate with an impressive residence on the right, standing high above the meadow. Over the next stile the

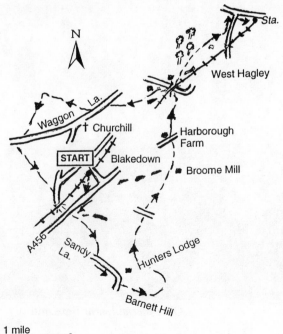

way passes a large pool on the left with swans and waterfowl, then through a kissing gate and over a railing stile.

Turn sharp left here onto a lane, passing an old forge on the right, (pool still on the left). Where the lane peters out into a field, turn right

Old watermill, near Brakemill

to pass along a narrow hedged way and over a stile into another pleasant meadow. Go straight across to a lane, then left to reach the picturesque village of Churchill. The church was built in 1867 on the site of a thirteenth century structure.

Take the footpath opposite the church, passing Old Churchill Farm House on the left and restored cottages on the right to climb a stile leading into a field. Turn sharp left and strike uphill, keeping the hedge on the left to another stile in the top corner. Bear right in the next field to pass a lone thorn bush, and continue on the same heading over a grassy knoll, pausing to admire the view, with Churchill nestling in its leafy hollow. From here the path continues on the same bearing to a waymarker on a wire fence. Turn left along the edge of field to a gate, leading onto a green lane. Continue along here, between hedges, to a second T-junction of paths, then turn left onto another green lane to reach Waggon Lane after half a mile.

Turn right, then left after about 200 yds onto a track which is fairly rough and follows a gully, with a golf course on the left, until Churchill Lane is reached. Turn left here, then right to arrive at Blakedown railway station.

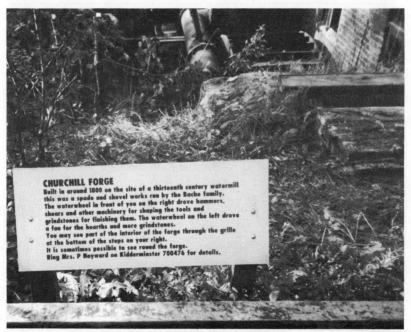

Remains of the old forge, Churchill

The Devil's Spittleful and Dowles Brook

by Norman Bradley

Maps: Landranger 138; Pathfinder 952 and 953
Start: Safari Park (G.R. 806759)
Finish: Bewdley (Bridge) (G.R. 786754)
Length of ramble: 8 miles; shorter version: 6 miles, starting and finishing at Blackstone Picnic Area (G.R. 796743) – *see footnote* *
Transport: M.R.W. 192 (Bus Station to Safari Park)
Parking: Track alongside Safari Park (1¼miles from Bewdley)
Terrain: easy – flat – forestry tracks and river path
Special feature: rock formation (Devil's Spittleful)
Ramble recommended at rhododendron time; also for autumn colours.
Refreshments: Cafés and Pubs at Bewdley

ALIGHT at the Safari Park and take the sandy track to the left of the entrance to the Park. Proceed for about half a mile before passing a signpost to the Devil's Spittleful. Ignore the first main bridle track and continue for a further 200 yds until a junction of paths is reached. Turn right here, then after a few yards, right again, to follow a narrow winding track leading to an amazing rock formation.

Climb the steps onto the top of the Devil's Spittleful to admire the view, before retracing your steps to the foot of the rock. Turn right and continue on the track, contouring the rocky outcrop for approx. 300 yds. Take the left-hand fork and follow the path, bearing left to reach the main track. Turn left and proceed, passing under the Severn Valley Railway to emerge on a lane. Turn right here and follow the lane under a disused railway to reach the bypass. Almost opposite, to the left of a lane, is Blackstone Picnic Site and Car Park. *(See footnote).

---

*   *Car drivers could park here at Blackstone Picnic Area and follow the scheduled walk from there and along the river to Bewdley, through the Wyre Forest to Dowles Brook, then the river path back to Bewdley. Continue along the river, retracing your steps to Blackstone. (Approximately 6 miles circular).*

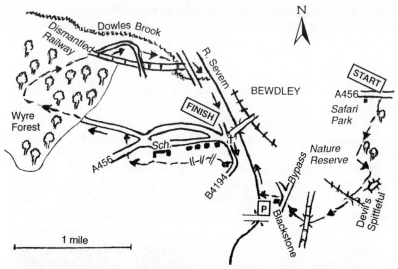

Turn right and cross carefully over the bypass, then continue until a track to a cottage is reached, signposted Netherton Lane. Follow this to the River Severn. Turn right on the riverside path, crossing a footbridge after a short distance, to continue on the path beside the river into Bewdley, (old Norman name 'Beaulieu' means beautiful place). At this point the Severn is spanned by Telford's three arched bridge, completed in 1801.

After crossing the river bridge walk along the main street which contains some stately old timber-framed houses, and pass to the left of the church (eighteenth century). Turn left at the top and continue along the road to where there is a sharp bend (ignoring Worcestershire Way signs). Take a drive on the right, running alongside the grounds of a large house 'Kateshill', which can be seen to the left. 'Kateshill' was the home of the late Dr Hicken, a former pupil of Westminster Road School, Handsworth, who became a world famous entomologist. The house was named after his wife. Continue along the path to reach a kissing gate. In the meadow beyond, proceed on a grassy track, keeping near the right-hand edge along the fence. Then after 100 yds turn right over a stile, along a fenced path (waymarked) to a footbridge over a stream, then through woodland leading to a residential road.

Cross over, turn left and take a gully on the right near the end house to reach another quiet road. Cross, then bear right to a signposted way, beside an electricity sub-station, to another residential road. Immediately opposite, a gully runs between houses and leads to a stile into a field. Go straight ahead here along a well defined path across the field, turning right at a hedge and bearing left at the top of the field to pass school grounds. Continue for about 200 yds, with open views on the left, and farm buildings ahead, until the hedge bears right. Follow it to the corner of the field and climb a stile by a bungalow onto the road.

Cross over, bear right and after a few yards take a drive on the left by a house and a hydrant sign. This follows a hedged way to a stile into a caravan site. Veer slightly right to follow a waymark down a tarmac track through the site, passing a children's play area. Bear left at the bottom to a gully over a stream into a lane. Turn left here and walk the length of the lane. Shortly after a cattle grid, turn right to enter the Wyre Forest on a waymarked track. Bear left, then fork right to follow downhill into the forest and continue to reach Dowles Brook. Follow the brook along to the right, passing pools, ignoring a footbridge on the

The Severn at Bewdley

right, and crossing stepping stones at one point, before continuing on the main track beside the brook. (Notice the remains of a charcoal burning site to the side of the path).

Near the end of a pool, the path veers right to climb uphill. Take the path on the left, halfway up, to go over a disused railway. Drop down onto the drive leading to 'Knowles Mill', turn right to join a lane and continue to a sign on the left to Fred Dale Nature Reserve. Turn along this path and follow it to pass Dowles Manor, once a beautiful half-timbered house until fire damaged it a few years ago.

When the main B4194 is reached turn right, then after a few yards, cross the road to climb a metal stile. Follow the path from here to the river, turning right on a riverside path into Bewdley. (M.R.W. Bus 192 returns to Birmingham).

The Fox Hunt Trail

by Mary Wall and Tom Birch

Maps: Landranger 139; Pathfinder 933
Start & Finish: Hayley Green (G.R. 949822) – circular walk
Finish: Gannow (G.R. 979783) *or* Rubery (G.R. 990773) – linear alternatives
Length of rambles: circular 8 miles (7 miles if shorter alternative is chosen). Linear: 8 miles (Gannow), 9 miles (Rubery)
Transport from Birmingham: M.R.W. 192 or W.M.T. 19 bus to the Fox Hunt (Hayley Green) on outward journey (return – circular)
W.M.T. 61 from Gannow (return). W.M.T. 63 from Rubery (return)
Terrain: Undulating – hilly in several places
Points of Interest: Trig point on Walton Hill; Toposcope on Adam's Hill; open views from above and from Calcot and Waseley Hills
Parking: Fox Hunt (circular walk)
Refreshments: Waseley and Nimmings Visitors' Centres; Manchester Inn and Fox Hunt

---

THE RAMBLE begins at the Fox Hunt, two stops after Lutley Lane. From the bus stop cross the road and turn right towards the traffic island, crossing with care, before turning left for about 100 yds to take a signposted footpath. (Ignore the first footpath to Clent sign). The path bears diagonally left across a field and through a gap in the bushes to climb a stile into Uffmoor Lane. Turn right here, then after about 200 yds take a tarmac track leading to Tack Farm. At the cattle grid a waymarked stile on the right leads into a field bordering Uffmoor Wood. (Uffmoor is said to take its name from Offa, King of Mercia in the eighth century).

Keeping near the edge of the wood, the path curves to the left, then goes straight ahead over three stiles before turning sharp right. The route is waymarked at regular intervals and continues with Uffmoor Wood on the right, until the field path bears left towards a ruined barn in the hedge. Here two stiles close together lead into another field rising uphill. Make for a large oak tree, stile adjacent, then bear left to a squeeze-stile in a left-hand hedge. Pass through and continue on the same heading to pass a gap in the next hedge, following marker poles to another squeeze-stile on the left of a large pool, where a grassy bank provides a good lunch spot.

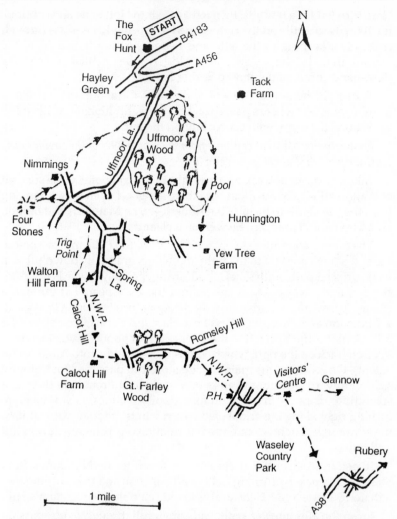

From here follow marker poles along the right-hand hedge to a stile which leads through a dingle, with a steep bank on the right, to another stile. Keep on the same heading until a stile is reached in the right-hand hedge, just before Yew Tree Farm. Follow along the left-hand hedge to another stile, then bear diagonally right across the next field to a corner stile.

Turn right on the lane for a few yds, then left at a footpath sign, crossing two fields before reaching a hedge and cross track. Turn right here and continue with the hedge on the left, until a farm is reached.

Here turn left for a few yds, then left again into Holt Lane and continue for 100 yds to a stile on the right signed to 'Spring Lane'. Pass through two fields, keeping to the left-hand hedge, bearing half right in the second field to drop down to a hidden stile in bushes near the right-hand corner and out onto Spring Lane.

Turn right here to a T-junction, then left for about 150 yds along Rumbow Lane to where a paved track on the right climbs steadily uphill to Walton Hill Farm, with Calcot Hill on the left.

For the linear walk now continue from ❀ on page 39. For the circular walk continue from the following paragraph.

Take a wide grass track bearing right to the trig point at the summit of Walton Hill (1,035 ft). From here there are good open views, ranging from the Clee Hills to include the Abberleys, the Malverns and Bredon Hill. The Wrekin may also be seen on a clear day.

The ramble continues along the ridge of Walton Hill, until just before the end a track goes off to the right and winds gradually downhill on a well surfaced path, with seats for admiring the view towards Frankley Beeches and Romsley. Near the bottom the track bears left through a cluster of trees to pass an information board. Turn left along the lane to a T-junction at St. Kenelm's Pass near Harcourt Farm. To complete the full circular route turn left at the T-junction for about 25 yds then take a rough track on the right which climbs quite steeply onto Adam's Hill (Clent). On reaching the main track bear left to pass the 'Four Stones' and on towards a clump of trees on the skyline. From here there is a splendid panorama, detailed on topography plaques, to study before turning right along the bridle path which winds gradually downhill to the Nimmings. There is a café and information centre here, also car park and toilets.

If preferred a shorter route may be taken to the Nimmings from St. Kenelm's pass by turning right at a T-junction and then turning first left along a lane to the Centre. This avoids climbing onto Adam's Hill.

From the Nimmings a path leads downhill through fields, passing through three gates *en route*, with good views of Wychbury Hill and the Hagley area opening up ahead. At the bottom turn right onto a grass track and continue to a narrow lane. Cross straight over and keeping a hedge on the left follow a field path, until two stiles are reached.

For the short route take the left-hand stile, dropping down on a field path to Lutley Lane on the main Kidderminster Road, near the start of ramble. The bus stops are to the right of an exit stile on the opposite side of the road.

To complete the full circular route, take the facing stile instead of the left-hand one, and keep the hedge on the left in the first field. Bear left for about 20 yds, then turn sharp right to go along a narrow track bordered by a high fence to the right and trees to the left. After a further 150 yds a stile on the right leads onto a narrow path and then onto a tarmac drive. Turn left and continue towards a farm, but do not pass through the main gate. Instead, turn left between low fence rails for a few yds to a waymarked stile. This leads into a meadow, with a duck pond on the right and an attractive modern farm building in pleasant surroundings.

Keep straight ahead to another stile, then bear right in the next field to follow a grassy bank with a stream on the right. Continue straight ahead, then bear right just before farm buildings to a stile in the right-hand hedge. This leads into Uffmoor Lane, where turn left and continue down the lane, passing Uffmoor Farm, to a stile on the left. Cross diagonally across the field and over a stile onto the main road, turning left to a traffic island and the Fox Hunt where the ramble began.

❧ THE LINEAR ROUTE

On reaching Walton Hill Farm, at the top of the paved track, turn left over a stile into a field. Follow the high level path (N.W.P.) along the ridge of Calcot Hill, a favourite spot on the Clent Hills. There are ever-changing views as the path winds and undulates, and one may be tempted to 'sit and rest awhile' on one of several seats, all of which are well positioned for admiring the scenery.

At a stile, just before Calcot Hill Farm, once the Manor of Richard de Caldcote, turn left downhill. Cross another stile, before dropping steeply down a grassy ridge onto Shutmill Lane. Turn right here, then left onto a lane, which is steep initially, but becomes more gradual as it passes Great Farley Wood. At the top turn right into Farley Lane, then after 100 yds take a signposted path on the left to follow through several fields, with distant view of the Malverns on the right. A stile at the bottom leads onto the B4551 near the Manchester Inn.

Turn right and cross to a lane on the left. This leads over a footbridge above the M5 motorway and continues to reach Chapman Hill Farm. Turn left here to follow a lane which bends right to pass cottages. Shortly afterwards a track goes off to the right. After climbing a stile, follow the left-hand hedge to reach two further stiles. From here the Visitors' Centre at Waseley Country Park can be seen to the left at the bottom of the next field.

On leaving the Centre take a surfaced track going to the right through the car park. This soon becomes a broad green track as it follows a fenced way to the left, emerging on Gannow Green Lane. Opposite is Boleyn Road and from a bus stop on the right-hand side the W.M.T. 61 returns to the City.

If preferred, from the Visitors' Centre, the walk may be extended by taking the track up onto Windmill Hill at the Gannow end of the Waseley Hills. Follow the main grass track along the ridge, passing the trig point and admiring the views. It dips and rises again before a track to the left drops down steeply to a car park and out onto a road near the bridge over the A38. Do not cross the bridge, but continue on a minor road, then under a subway to join a main road leading through the shopping area at Rubery. Continue past a church on the right, to a bus stop on the left a little further on. From here the W.M.T. 63 may be caught, also M.R.W. 143, back to the City.

Waseley Hills Visitors' Centre
Hereford & Worcester Countryside Service

Castle Hill and Kinver

by Lilian Bowron

Maps: Landranger 138; Pathfinder 933
Start: Kinver High Street(G.R. 845836)
Finish: Bus at Meddins Lane (near terminus 242) (G.R. 837838)
Length of ramble: 8 miles
Transport: Train from Birmingham (New Street) to Stourbridge
Junction; then rail shuttle to Stourbridge Town, *or* W.M.T. No. 9 bus to
Stourbridge bus station, then W.M.T No. 242 bus to Kinver
Parking: Off Kinver High Street and at Comber Road
Terrain: Hilly, two climbs (not strenuous)
Refreshments: Inns and cafés in Kinver

THE WALK starts from the bus stop at Kinver, outside the Community Health Centre in the High Street. From there walk to the left for 100 yds, then turn right along a passageway beside Kings Court Restaurant, to pass a car park on the left. A path leads from here, rising steadily to begin with, until a waymarked cross path is reached. Turn right here and continue uphill on an easier gradient, bearing to the right at the top onto a tarmac road.

Here turn left and follow uphill, pausing to admire the view down over the town and beyond, before passing the church – a prominent landmark. At a T-junction turn right into Church Road and continue for approx. 400 yds to Comber Road (car park here). Go straight ahead to enter the National Trust area on Kinver Edge and follow a broad track along the tree line to the left. This dips and then rises until it levels out near an open hut in the trees ahead, where the route bears left onto a sandy track which runs beside a wire fence on the left. From here there are good open views, looking back to the Clent Hills.

When the wire fence ends, turn sharp left at horse barriers and continue downhill due south, on this track, for about three quarters of a mile. Ignore all cross tracks and pass through more horse barriers to join a bridle path, just before reaching the lane at Blakeshall.

Turn right on the lane for a few yards, then right again along a narrow path, crossing the drive of Blakeshall Hall. The path continues straight ahead beside a holly hedge on the right to a lane. Here turn right and follow the lane as it swings slightly left and continue to a 'No Through Road' sign leading to Solcum Farm. Take this route, passing

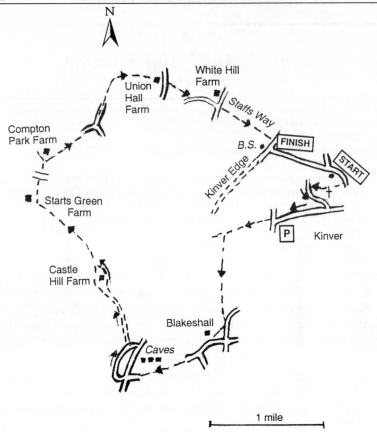

Moat Court Farm on the right, then straight on for another 200 yds to a stile on the right of a cottage. This leads into a sheltered gully, near the end of which can be seen evidence of rock houses on the cliff to the right, before reaching Kingsford Lane. These were inhabited for about 400 years, until the middle of the present century.

Cross the road into Sladd Lane and take the first turning on the right at New House Farm. Continue to a road junction, where take the left of two bridleways signed to 'Starts Green', climbing steadily at first, then more steeply up to Castle Hill Farm. Keep to the right of buildings by turning right through a gate and straight ahead on a field path, with a meadow sloping away to the right. Climb a stile to rejoin the main track, turning right after about 100 yds to follow along a well defined track, with open fields on the left at this point. After a short distance the track narrows and follows along a ridge for approximately one mile,

The Old School House, Kinver

with occasional glimpses of the view on either side as gaps appear in the hedge and bracken.

The track ends by a house at Starts Green, where turn right onto a slightly broader track to join a farm drive which leads onto a road. Cross straight over onto the drive of Compton Park Farm, and where the drive divides turn right through a gate onto a waymarked path. Continue downhill to another gate and from here veer slightly right with the main track, passing a barn and through a further gate on the right. Then keeping to the left-hand hedge go straight down to a stile at the bottom of the field into a plantation (N.T.). Follow a path through trees, crossing a steam and on leaving the woodland area a wide bridleway leads over several stiles before reaching a road.

Here turn left and just after passing Compton Hall Farm take a stile on the right, then keeping to the right-hand hedge veer right to another stile. In the next field bear left to reach a double stile near the corner, with the tip of woodland a few yards to the right. Climb stiles and turn right for about 10 yds before bearing 90° left to follow a line of trees. At the top turn right onto a broad track, which swings right after a short distance and continues with a hedge on the left to reach Union Hall

Farm. Pass straight through a large farmyard area, with barns on the right, leading to a road.

Turn right for 50 yds, then pick up a signposted path on the left into a field. The views are opening up now all round and ahead, with the whole length of Kinver Edge stretching to the right. Follow the left-hand hedge to the bottom of the first field, then follow the waymark sign, turning right in the same field to follow the hedge. Cross a stile in the left-hand corner and from here turn 90° right to a footpath sign onto a lane.

Turn left and proceed to a T-junction at Little Brook House, then straight across onto a track signed 'Staffs. Way', leading first through woodland, then across two fields to Meddins Lane. The No. 242 bus may be caught approx. 100 yds to the right to return to Stourbridge Town.

If wishing to return to Kinver village, turn right into Meddins Lane, then straight across through alleyways and a crescent to reach a busy road. Turn left downhill to reach the main road, where a right-hand turn leads into the village.

Old cave dwellings near Kinver

Abbots Castle Hill

by Gwen Langstone

Maps: Landranger 138 & 139; Pathfinder 912
Start and Finish: G.R. 871934
Length of ramble: 10 miles. Shorter routes: A–D (7½ miles); B–C (9 miles)
Public transport: Trains from Birmingham New Street to Wolverhampton or to Stourbridge Town (via junction) then by W.M.T. 256 bus from either of above. Alight in Wombourne at the corner of Station Road and Bull Meadow Lane
Car park: Adjacent to picnic area at Bratch Bridge (the ramble can be started and finished at this point) G.R. 867938
Terrain: fairly easy – one gentle climb but vegetation and crops can hinder progress during growing season
Refreshments: Inns at Seisdon, Trysull and N.W. of Foxlands Farm.

BUS PASSENGERS walk west along Mount Road. This quiet way runs onto a path which meanders right and then left around a sandpit. Climb a stile and go forward downhill across a meadow to climb a further stile. Here turn right to walk alongside the Staffs. & Worcs. Canal. Shortly go through the picnic area to the road at Bratch Bridge.

Before turning left along Bratch Lane take a few minutes and fifty paces right to admire the Victorian splendour of the pumping station built in 1895. Soon turn left along Bratch Common Road and take a stile on the right, some 20 yds beyond the gates of Little Woodford farmhouse. The path goes diagonally left across this field to a stile in the corner and continues in a second field alongside a left-hand hedge to a stile on the left. Follow the hedge on the right to climb a stile by a gate onto a lane.

Cross the lane and take the track opposite to Woodford Grange. At cross tracks, by a red brick barn, veer right to pass on the left a white house and a bungalow. Continue forward with the track to cross a stream and emerge back onto the lane.

Here turn left towards Hunters Green. Just before civilisation is reached turn left along a track which borders to the right the small Trysull Park, complete with picnic area. Continue for about one mile before reaching the Bridgnorth Road (B4176) and cross to a stile opposite. With a hedge on the left walk the length of an undulating field

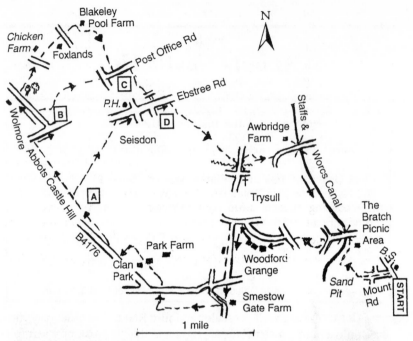

Victorian pumping station at Bratch

to emerge at a sharp bend on the lane beside Smestow Gate Farm.

Turn left for 50 yds, taking a stile on the right opposite Smestow Lane. Turn right along the hedge, then left at the corner of the same field to follow uphill, with the hedge still on the right, to a stile in the far hedge. Turn right, then left around the field corner, to regain your original heading. Pass farm barns and continue forward with a track to reach another stile and climb a flight of steps beyond onto a golf course (not shown on the current O.S. Map).

Here turn right for a few yards, then left in front of the 3rd 'green' to follow a waymarker leading between two clumps of trees. Just before another 'green' turn right at a marker post, then left after 50 yds, to aim for a small white building. Cross a surfaced path, keeping right of a white building and continue with care across a high fairway, going straight ahead to pass a tall black and white marker post on the right.

Take the signed path through a small copse to emerge on the main road. Cross to a stile opposite and proceed with a hedge on the left to

Bratch locks

begin with, then walk on the same heading across an open field, aiming for the red-bricked Clan Park Farm.

On reaching a track turn right to reach a rough farm drive. Here turn left and continue for approx. 250 yds along a green lane.

Opposite a gateway on the right, turn left through a small gap in the hedge and go forward in a SW direction, across a large field to a gap in the hedge onto a very busy main road.

Turn right along the B4176 and in a few yards take a track on the right. However, before disappearing into the trees to climb Abbots Castle Hill, pause to admire the view across the Severn Valley to the Clee Hills. As the hill is climbed one may still glimpse to the left, between the trees, stunning views of the Shropshire hills and to the right the not so beautiful Black Country and West Midland conurbation beyond.

After three quarters of a mile at cross paths the walk may be shortened at point A (see sketch map) by taking a green track going right (N.E.) for a further three quarters of a mile to a lane and then taking a right turn to Seisdon. Continue on the lane to pass the inn and over cross roads into Ebstree Road. Keep to the same direction for another half a mile to pass on the right the lane to Trysull.

Here rejoin the longer routes at point D on the sketch map. (Continue reading from ✤ on page 49.)

The longer routes continue along Abbots Castle Hill, going straight ahead at cross paths (point A), keeping as close as possible to the right-hand edge of trees. Ignore a path going down to the left and keep on the same heading to descend to the road by the side of a quaint castellated house called Tinker's Castle. Turn right along this busy road which leads to Seisdon. In a quarter of a mile a track on the left to Wolmore Farm is taken.

Here, after approx. 300 yds, the middle distance walk takes the clearly marked Staffs. Way signs on the right starting just beyond a lone portion of a very tall old holly hedge. (Point B). Otherwise continue reading from ✿ on page 49.

Go through a small gate in wooden fencing and follow the hedge on the left along an enclosed path, to a gap in the field corner. Turn left here, the hedge now on the right. After a short distance turn right at the field corner by wooden rails and continue with the hedge on the right for about 300 yds. Go through the gate onto a rough track and straight ahead, passing a farm on the left. In 300 yds the track swings left by an electricity sub-station. Turn sharp left here on a rough track which in another 80 yds emerges onto the road. Turn left, then immediately right down Post Office Road.

In a quarter of a mile, opposite houses numbered 150 and 148 turn right over a stile and rejoin the main walk (Point C). *Continue reading from* ❦ *below.*

❧ The longer walk continues from point B along the Wolmore Farm track passing a Staffs. Way sign, to turn right along a track which runs along the left hand side of a copse. At the end of trees, where the track turns right, continue on the same heading (30° bearing) aiming to the right of a distant grey-roofed building with a tower (rather like a silo). Find an old gateway gap in the hedge ahead and continue straight on to go through the far hedge. Cross a track to a small metal gate situated to the right of the grey-roofed farm building. Keep on the same heading to go through another gate in the far hedge, then onward through metal gates into Foxlands farmyard and straight ahead to the road.

If refreshment is required turn left for the Fox Inn, otherwise cross the road and go a few paces right to take a track to Blakeley Pool Farm. A little beyond an open metal-roofed barn turn right in front of the farmhouse to go over a stile into rough pasture. Walk with the boundary wall of the farmhouse garden on the left and when the path emerges into a larger field continue on the same heading with a hedge on the right. Go through another field and just before the corner turn right through a gate/stile.

Ignore a stile to the left and continue forward in a southerly direction until this path becomes a track and emerges onto Post Office Road. Turn left and after approx. 300 yds climb a stile on the right opposite houses 150 and 148 where the middle distance ramble rejoins at point C.

❦ The path continues through a field to a stile in the hedge ahead, then over another two fields to corner stiles, keeping the fence and brook below to the left. Here the path becomes enclosed between gardens, then follows the bank along – above a housing estate – to enter a rather superior garden. Just before reaching the house look for a stile on the left to the road.

Cross the road to a garden gate directly opposite and go through, keeping left of Mill House, to reach the road beyond. Turn left along Ebstree Road. The short walk rejoins the route at this point (D on sketch map).

❧ Pass Roost Farm and the large white 'Roost House' before turning right beside a house named 'At Last', continuing along an unsurfaced track to Trysull. In approximately one mile an old mill and bakehouse, now tastefully converted into upmarket homes, are passed to reach the lane at Trysull. The Bell and Plough Inns and church lie to the right.

The way goes left for a few yards to take a stile opposite, adjacent to the drive of 'Greenacres'. A track runs right of the house to a stile by a gate. The path then continues through a delightful meadow, complete with stream, to a fence stile near corner. Walk a few yards on the same heading, then climb diagonally left (N.E.) up this large field, passing to the right of a pylon and aiming for a gateway to the right of farm buildings.

Go straight ahead down the lane for 300 yds, then turn right to follow a scenic route along the canal tow path for about one mile, leaving the canal at Bratch Bridge. Turn left, and in a few yards, right through the picnic area.

For car drivers this is the end of ramble, but others will need to retrace their outward steps back to W.M.T. 256 near Bull Meadow Lane, to return to Wolverhampton or Stourbridge.

All Saints Church, Trysull

Walk 13
Wrottesley Park
by Beryl Harris.

Maps: Landranger 127; Pathfinder 891
Start: Codsall (GR 865037)
Finish: Perton (GR 857003)
Length of ramble: 9 miles
Transport: Train (New Street) to Wolverhampton; then WMT 535 from Bus Station (adjacent to railway station) to Codsall on outward journey. WMT 510 from Perton to Wolverhampton on return
Terrain: Fairly level and on good tracks
Special features: Good, open views on entering Wrottesley Park. Pendrell Hall * (see footnote)
Refreshments: The Summer House (P.H.) on A464 nr. Kingswood Common

FROM the bus stop, near the Crown Inn at Codsall, cross the main road and turn left into Church Road. Proceed to Codsall Church and through the churchyard onto a lane, where almost opposite is a footpath sign pointing downhill, past the cemetery. Follow this to enter a field, then with a hedge on left continue on the field path to cross a footbridge. Keep on the same heading to reach a stile at Nursery Farm, then straight ahead along the farm drive to a road.

Cross to a stile and continue with a hedge on the left to go over a right-hand stile near the corner of field. Proceed with the hedge on the left to cross two more stiles before emerging on the road. Turn left here, passing Pendrell Hall *(see footnote). On reaching a church on the corner of Whitehouse Lane bear left, then at a T-junction turn left again.

After 300 yds along the road take a track on the right to pass Woodhall Farm, a most attractive building in a delightful setting. There is evidence of the original moat, now only a pool in which water fowl

---

* *The Pendrell family sheltered King Charles II at Boscobel House after the Battle of Worcester. (Boscobel House was the hunting lodge). In gratitude, the King left a sum of money, to be paid annually to the Pendrell family, which is still paid to this day. In 1993 the amount was £49.47p after tax. This would have been worth quite a lot in King Charles' day.*

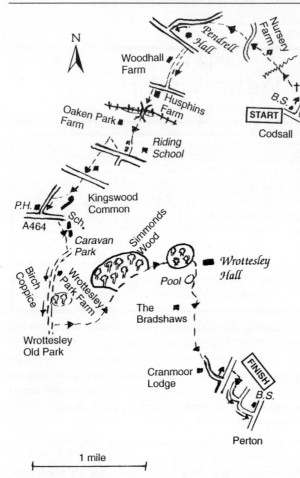

swim happily. On leaving this peaceful scene continue along the track and at the end turn right into Husphins Lane. After passing Husphins Farm, continue to a bend in the road, then take a field path on the left. Keeping the hedge on the left proceed to a stile, then go immediately left over another stile into the adjacent field. From here bear diagonally right to a gate in the fence near a bridge over the railway.

After crossing the railway bear right across the next field to the far corner where there are two stiles. Cross the left-hand stile and with a hedge on the right continue to the corner of the field, where an iron footbridge over a ditch leads into a small wood. The path passes several houses to emerge onto a track. Turn right and keep bearing right to a T-junction of paths (to the left is Oaken Riding School). Turn right again here and where the main track swings left, take a path on the right, with hedges on both sides to begin with. This opens out onto a field path, with Oaken Park Farm now in view to the right.

After another 200 yds look for a stile on the left, to the right of a metal gate, then with a hedge on the right go straight ahead to reach the main road (A41), passing farm buildings. Cross over to Kingswood Common picnic area. From the point of entry head due south across the picnic

Pendrell Hall

area, bearing left after about 25 yds onto a good track, just beyond two large oak trees on the left. This path goes through trees to join another path which skirts the grounds of a school on the left, then passes several houses as the path enters a lane. At a T-junction turn left and follow along this road to reach the A464 (The Summer House P.H. is on the right). A Shropshire boundary sign can be seen on the opposite side of the road.

Turn left here for about 75 yds, then cross over to take a long, narrow woodland path which rises steadily and passes near to a permanent caravan site on the left. On reaching a surfaced track turn right, from which point a splendid panorama opens up to the west. The view ranges from the Wrekin on the far right and includes Ironbridge Power Station, the Clee Hills and extends to the Abberleys. The track leads to Wrottesley Farm and after some 300 yds, just past Birch Coppice, a good track goes off to the left. Follow this and, on reaching a cross track, turn left again along the edge of trees, then, after 40 yds, sharp left to follow alongside Simmonds Wood.

At the end of woodland turn right onto a surfaced track and continue to a T-junction of trees, opposite a cottage on the right. Here turn left to walk alongside the drive to Wrottesley Hall. Continue on this track, following the lake around until a path turns left, then after about 150 yds look for an arrow indicating a field path to the right. Follow this and go straight ahead with the hedge on the left, until a path from the Bradshaws comes in from the right.

Here go through a gap in the hedge on the left and continue on the same heading, with a hedge now on the right, to reach farm buildings at Cranmoor Lodge. Turn left here, in front of the farm, then swing right at the end of buildings onto a lane which leads down to the main road near Perton. There is a small nursery on the left.

To avoid the busy main road into Perton, turn left for a few yards and cross to a track opposite the nursery, which runs beside houses. Follow the right-hand boundary fence into Hoylake Road (cul-de-sac), then go right again into St Andrew's Drive at the end of which turn left along the main road. The bus stop (W.M.T. 510) to return to Wolverhampton is approx. 25 yds from here.

Remains of the moat around Woodhall Farm

Fairoak Valley, Cannock Chase
by Bert Wilson

> Maps: Landranger 127 and 128; Pathfinder 871 and 872
> Start and finish: Hednesford (G.R. 000125)
> Length of ramble: 9 miles
> Transport from Birmingham: Train (New Street) to Hednesford
> Parking: At Hednesford, adjacent to Railway Station, Bus Station and Valley Heritage Centre
> Refreshments: Inn at Hazelslade ¼ mile diversion from ❋ in text
> Terrain: Fairly easy on woodland tracks and open moorland with some gradual climbs

ASCEND the steps from Hednesford railway station and enter Market Street. Turn right, then take the first turn on the left into the bus station (Victoria Street). Continue straight ahead, then where the road goes sharp right, enter a gate into Hednesford Park. Follow the path through the park which goes right to pass tennis courts and a bowling green to emerge on the Rugeley Road (A460).

Go over this road and turn left, then first right into Valley Road. Continue past the Valley Heritage Centre (car park available) and straight forward through the right-hand gate. Where the tracks cross, after about 200 yds, turn left uphill, bearing right at a signpost and over open moorland (62°) to reach a ditch. Walk alongside this for a few yards, before turning left at a junction of paths, and continue straight ahead on a grassy track towards a wooded hill. This track drops steeply down to Rawnsley Road.

Go forward into Rugeley Road, opposite, then where it bends right (❋ near Hazelslade), turn left up a broad track between houses to pass a track on the left and continue to a T-junction where a well defined track can be seen. Here turn right uphill, with a golf course on the left, reaching the Club House in approximately three-quarters of a mile. The path goes straight ahead, with the Club House on the right, then after a short ascent goes downhill in a northerly direction, with splendid views opening up. After about a mile the path bears left to the main road, passing a signpost on the right and a pumping station to the left.

Go over the A460 and straight forward, to continue along Marquis Drive, named after the Marquis of Anglesey. The route crosses the railway line and climbs steadily uphill. This section of the Drive was

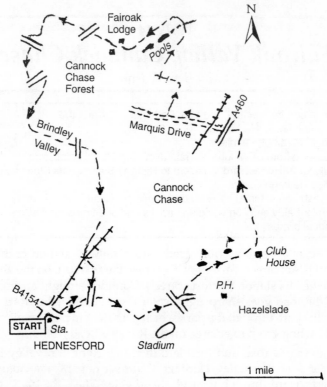

known as 'Kit Bag Hill' during the War, but today walkers carry nothing heavier than rucksacks!

After approximately half a mile take a grassy track on the right, where telegraph wires start (Pole No. FCTC 11). Following a short ascent, the path levels out and meets a cross track. Ignore this and go straight ahead, passing a grassy open space on the left and good views to the right, (east and south east).

Where the path enters the woods, about 500 yds after leaving Marquis Drive, turn left at a 'Danger' sign and continue on a well defined track, disregarding the first cross track. At the next cross track turn right on a wide track leading downhill, until after 700 yds it joins a main track. Go left here and continue over the stream using stepping stones, then bear left to pass a 'Forest Nature Reserve' sign.

The route continues past Fairoak Valley pools on the left, an ideal spot for a picnic lunch. After passing the last big pool, continue for about 200 yds to a junction of tracks, with a small pond on the left. Here turn sharp right up a steep bank, bearing right at the top to Fairoak

Lodge. Turn left between the houses, with a conifer hedge on the right to begin with, and follow this track to reach a road after a short distance.

Go over the road and straight ahead to a caravan/camp site, turning left to go down the main line of sites, branching right before the end to join a surfaced track. Turn left onto this track (bearing 205°) which is broad, straight and surfaced. This leads to a lane. Go straight forward here onto a woodland path leading downhill, then after approx. 200 yds turn left at the next cross track to reach another lane. Cross over and enter a small car park to the left, then go forward for about 50 yds to take a right-hand fork. This goes downhill at first, then up for a short distance before reaching a waymarked cross track (No. 7) after about half a mile from the car park.

Here go left, descending to a minor road in Brindley Valley. Turn right, cross over and take the lower track in the Country Park, which bears right to run parallel with the road. Continue for about a mile on pleasant paths and passing pools, before joining the main road near the railway bridge. Turn left, using the pedestrian way over the bridge, then turn right onto the A460. Walk along this road to reach the gate into Hednesford Park on the right. Retrace your steps through the park and bus station to arrive back at the railway station in Market Street.

Farewell to Elmhurst
by Tom Webster

Maps: Landranger 128; Pathfinder 872 and 892
Start & Finish: Lichfield (G.R. 119091)
Length of ramble: 9½ miles
Transport from Birmingham: Train (New Street) to Lichfield City *or*
Stevensons Bus No. 112 from Birmingham (Edgbaston St.) to Lichfield
Bus Station
Parking: Lichfield city centre *or* Beacon Park (start from ❀ below)
Terrain: Undulating – fairly easy
Special features: Lichfield old city, including the cathedral
Refreshments: Curborough Hall Farm (slight detour *en route*), and
Lichfield city centre.

O N LEAVING the railway station, almost opposite the bus station, turn left for 100 yds to traffic lights. Cross over, turning right into St. John Street and continue straight ahead. (Note the plaque on the wall on the right indicating one of four city gates and Bishop Roger de Clinton). Follow through a traffic-free zone and into Bird Street, walking towards the cathedral and passing the Arts Centre on the right.

Cross the main road to enter the main gate into Beacon Park, leaving the cathedral behind and notice the statue of the captain of the Titanic on the left of the main path. Continue on this path to reach a single bar metal barrier at a small car park.

❀ *Beacon Park car park*

Turn right onto a tarmac path to pick up a hedge on the right, veering left to cross the main road onto another path leading to the corner of a residential road. Go straight ahead here, passing Christchurch primary school and almost immediately take a path on the right, running between wire fences and alongside the school grounds. This ends in a cul-de-sac, where you turn left towards garages. Turn right here to pass in front of the garages, to pick up a path going half left across two small fields to reach a bridlepath alongside a wood.

Here turn right and follow the bridlepath which swings left to enter the wood, passing a cottage, then continues for approx. 250 yds until just before a large residence a right-hand fork leads to an exit stile from the wood. Walk towards another woodland area (middle distance) and a left-hand double H.T. pylon. After crossing a brook follow a path, keeping

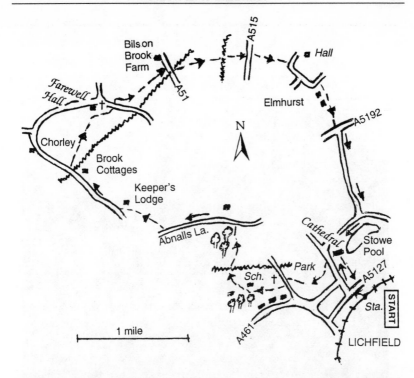

parallel with the wood on the left (now on the Heart of England Way). At a point where a hedge joins the wood climb a stile to follow a path through to a lane (Abnalls Lane). Watch out for deer in the parkland on the left beyond the wood.

On reaching Abnalls Lane turn left and continue for about two thirds of a mile to a stile on the right (H.O.E.W.). Cross a first field half left to a stile, then proceed on the same heading (300°) to the corner of the next field, leaving a farm well to the left. Where the fence joins a hedge, cross the stile and follow with the hedge on the left to cross a brook, then with the hedge still on the left aim for a stile in the facing hedge. Continue straight ahead from here to a corner stile onto the lane, left of Keeper's Lodge and continue forward along the lane to take the right-hand fork to Chorley, passing Brook Cottage on the right.

An easier alternative from this point (to avoid crops which can impede progress on the right-of-way) would be to continue along the lane after passing Brook Cottage until crossroads are reached. A right-hand turn here leads to Farewell Hall. (Now continue reading from ❋ on page 60.)

Lichfield Cathedral

If no problems with crops are expected then immediately after crossing a bridge over a brook look for a stile in the right-hand hedge and proceed up a field, with conifers on the right, to a stile and then straight ahead in the next field to another stile (where the hedge meets a brook and a ditch). Cross here, keeping near to a brook on the right to look for a marker sign on the fence. The right of way now goes diagonally half left across the field, following a line of telegraph posts, until it joins a path near the church in the top right-hand corner; here it swings right to a stile in the right-hand hedge. Farewell Hall is on the left near the church.

❀ Here turn right along the lane, passing Mill Farm to reach a gap in the hedge on the left, just before a bridge over the stream. Keeping the stream on the right in the first field make for another rather narrow gap in the facing hedge, then follow to a stile in the corner of the second field, approaching Bilston Brook Farm. Cross the stile and keep to the left of a bank to join a farm track, where you turn right over the brook and then left to the main road (A51).

Cross over and look for a hidden stile in the hedge (half left), then with a hedge on the left keep straight ahead to the end of the field to where a wire fence is cut and looped for access. Continue on the same heading in the next field to a corner stile, then half right to cross over a brook on a sleeper bridge. From here bear left to an old metal gate/fence. Cross this and go straight ahead, aiming for a large oak tree and hedge line. With the hedge on the left walk uphill to pass a pool on the left, then diagonally right to a gap near the corner of the field to emerge on the A515.

Cross over, bearing half left to a stile, then straight ahead in a field to a gap in the corner. Keeping a hedge on the right, proceed for a short distance, passing a small pool on the left to reach a stile to the left of a gate. This leads onto a track and out onto a bend in the road (Lodge on left). Continue straight ahead here for about 300 yds and where the road bends to the left a stile on the right leads across a field and between houses onto Fox Lane where you turn right. However, it is worth visiting the nearby hamlet of Elmhurst with its quaint cottages and Mission House. This may be reached by continuing along the lane from the Lodge and bearing right to reach Fox Lane.

Follow this lane until a footpath signed 'Only To Left' is reached and follow this to reach a hedge line, with the cathedral now clearly visible on the skyline. This is unique in that it possesses three spires which are known as 'Ladies of the Vale'.

Continue straight ahead with the hedge on the left to pass through a kissing gate in the hedge to enter the adjacent field. From here the path goes diagonally left to cross a footbridge, where a left-hand turn leads to the main road. Cross half right into Curborough Road and follow for approximately three quarters of a mile until the Oakleigh Hotel appears on the right.

At the end of the hotel wall a track on the right goes alongside Stowe Pool. Follow this and continue on the same heading to a T-junction at the 'Close'. (There is an opportunity to visit the cathedral at this point, which is historically interesting and dates back to the reign of Edward I). From the wall of the close turn left towards the city centre to pass a small pool and a church on the right, where a statue of James Boswell can be seen.

Turn right into the traffic-free area, passing the Guildhall on the left and Tourist Information Office, then through an archway on the left into the main shopping area. Turn right at the end of the street, then left towards traffic lights. The railway station is diagonally left across the main road. *If returning to Beacon Car Park continue reading from the first paragraph.*

Walk 16
Beside Black Brook
by Joan Bamber

Maps: Landranger 139; Pathfinder 892
Start: Blake Street (G.R. 106008)
Finish: Lower Bangley (G.R. 174017)
Length of ramble: 6½ miles
Transport from Birmingham: Train (New Street) to Blake Street (*outward*); M.R.N. bus from Lower Bangley (Nr Mile Oak) (*return*)
Refreshments: Pub at Little Hay
Terrain: relatively flat, easy walking

FROM the main exit of the Railway Station at Blake Street, turn left and follow the road past the Blakebarn pub to a T-junction. Cross the road and continue to the crossroads at Watford Gap. Here turn left, cross over the main road and continue for approx. 400 yds, passing the Highwayman pub. Then, a few yards past the next group of houses, turn right at a footpath sign into a field.

Go ahead with the power lines to the left and cross two fields, first with the hedge on the left, then the right, to reach a stile into a third field. Continue ahead with Alder Farm to the right and over another two stiles onto a lane.

Turn left and walk through Little Hay village. Just beyond the telephone box on the right, opposite a row of cottages, cross a stile hidden in the hedge. Go ahead to cross a stile, a footbridge over a stream and two further stiles, always keeping the hedge on the left, to enter a wood. With an impressive residence on the left, follow the gravel track to go through a metal gate beside two houses and continue downhill between two quarries to reach a lane. Pause *en route* to look left where the view extends to Shenstone church.

Turn right and walk along the lane, where rhododendrons bloom in June, until on the left there is a sign to 'Thick Broom House'. Here is the first sighting of Black Brook, but the way continues on the lane to a junction at the A38.

Cross the two carriageways and turn right, passing Black Brook farmhouse, then after another few yards turn left through the farmyard. Here bear right to go under the power lines onto a field track, with views opening up on either side and ahead. At the end of track turn left along a farm track, which becomes a lane at 'Weeford Stables'. After crossing the Brook, bear right on the lane to a road.

Turn right along the road, then right again into the car park of the 'School House' restaurant. (Opposite is Weeford church, which is worth

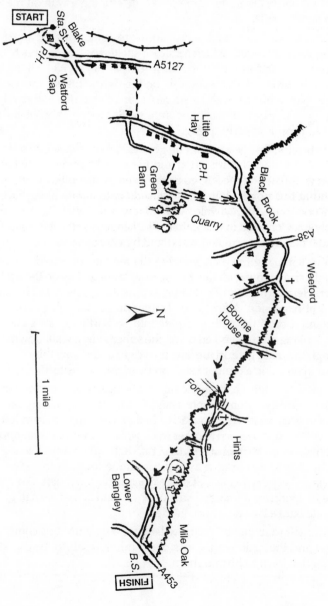

a visit). Continue the walk by keeping close to the restaurant and at the end of the building enter a field. Go straight ahead, keeping the fence on the left, to follow along a bank, on a raised path above a meadow to the right, where Black Brook flows steadily on its course. Climb a stile into the next field and walk in the same direction, gaining a wall on the right to reach another stile.

Cross the driveway of 'Bourne House' to a stile opposite and go ahead through a small wood, which affords a sheltered spot for lunch. Go over another drive and turn right to follow footpath signs, along a track which crosses the brook, with the 'House' on the right. This is a most attractive setting, with a bridge over the stream, a small waterfall and overhanging trees, especially beautiful at blossom time. Snowdrops and celandines are an added bonus in early spring.

On leaving this peaceful scene go ahead over a stile into a large field and after a few yards turn left at another stile. Keeping to the field edge, with a wire fence on the left, go ahead to enjoy the rolling countryside all around at this point. Shortly a stile leads onto a path along the edge of pinewoods on the right, while two fields away to the left Black Brook flows quietly on. Continue over another stile, keeping to the left-hand fence in the next field to enter mixed woodland by way of a stile.

Turn left along the path, viewing the remains of an old watermill on the right and follow with the 'Brook' now immediately on the left to reach a lane. Here turn left and continue to pass the gateway to Hints Hall on the right-hand side. A few yards further on go through a clearing in the trees and ascend the path to a gate into St. Bartholomew's churchyard. After looking around and enjoying the superb view, walk down the steps through the main gate. In the lane turn right and follow this for about 400 yds until reaching a footpath sign on the right, opposite 'Botley House'.

Follow the sign, crossing the Brook for the last time on this walk, then turning left at a waymarker into a field. Continue along the left-hand hedge until the track veers right to reach a hedge and tree line. Turn left here to follow the hedge to reach another track which winds past a signpost. Aim for the corner of the trees ahead, then turn half right on an ancient cart track which leads to a stile near a farm. Continue towards the edge of farm buildings, keeping inside the field to reach a stile on the left. Cross the farm drive to another waymarked stile opposite and across a small field to an exit stile onto a lane near farm garden.

Turn left to follow this narrow lane for a mile until reaching Bangley House and the main road. Cross over and walk left to the bus stop and M.R.N. 110 back to Birmingham.

Dumble Wood
by Ted and Joyce Jones

Maps: Landranger: 139; Pathfinder: 935 and 914
Start & Finish: Coleshill High Street. G.R. 201890
Length of ramble: 9 miles
Transport from Birmingham: W.M.T. 90 bus to Coleshill High Street
near church entrance
Parking: Off High Street
Terrain: Easy: fairly flat: mainly using lanes and field paths
Special feature: Picturesque village at Church End in lovely rural setting
Refreshments: available in Coleshill and at the Griffin Inn (an
eighteenth century hostelry) at Church End

A LIGHT at the lych gate entrance to the parish church in Coleshill High Street. Walk up the path to the church, bearing right to follow the path through the churchyard leading into the cemetery. Here bear right again to follow the hedge line to a metal kissing gate. Cross a track to another kissing gate, then go across the corner of a field to climb a stile, near a seat. From here follow a well defined track downhill to a fence, then cross a ditch and follow the track to a bridge over the river Blythe.

Continue along this track for about half a mile towards the golf course, passing Castle Farm and a pool on the right. On reaching the golf course cross a stile and follow the right-hand fence. A distant view of Maxstoke Castle can be seen through the trees on the left. It is still lived in by the Fetherston-Dilke family, who have been there since 1599.

The path continues between two pools and bears slightly right to a stile in the hedge. Climb this and keeping the hedge on the left continue for about 150 yds to another stile on the left which leads back onto the edge of the golf course. From the stile cross the corner, keeping to the right of mature oak trees to reach a stile in the hedge, leading onto a lane.

Turn left for a short distance to Dumble Farm drive on the right and proceed along this drive until a stile is reached on the left, near some tall poplar trees, just before farm buildings. Climb this and follow the path across the field to the edge of a wood, leaving Dumble Farm on the right. (An attractive residence built in 1595). At the hedge corner cross a stile, and with the hedge on the left continue in the next field to

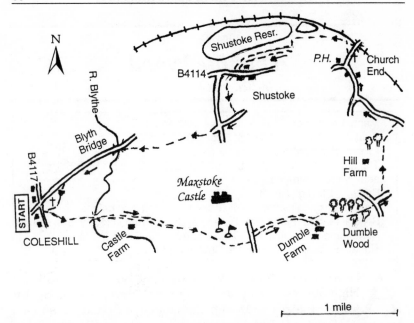

1 mile

go over the stile straight ahead, ignoring the one on the left. Follow around the left-hand edge of the field to another stile leading into Dumble Wood, where a grassy track leads through a delightful stretch of woodland for a few hundred yards, before crossing a plank bridge and out onto a lane.

Almost opposite, the lane forks right towards Fillongley. Follow this and after approx. 300 yds look for a stile in the left-hand hedge near a pylon. Climb this stile and with the field hedge on the left continue for 100 yds before turning left just before the pylon onto a waymarked path. Turn right almost immediately to follow with a hedge on the right in this field. (Hill Farm can be seen to the left across field). After about 300 yds look for a waymark sign on the right leading into the next field, crossing a plank bridge. Turn left to follow the left-hand hedge to a lane.

Here turn left, noticing Dawmill colliery on the right, and in the distance the spire of Over Whitacre church. Ahead Shustoke parish church can be seen amidst trees. Follow the lane to a road junction, and turn right, continuing along the lane towards Church End, passing the Old Rectory (this was the birthplace of Sir William Dugdale, the well-known seventeenth century antiquarian). Just before the next road junction turn right to visit St. Cuthbert's church, where a walk around the churchyard to admire the views in every direction is to be recommended.

From here follow the track on the left of the church to a wooden kissing gate, then continue on a field path to go through a wooden gate onto the busy B4114. Turn left and cross the road then, just past Watson Petroleum, turn right and cross a stile on the right. Follow a field path alongside the hedge and river, ignoring a path under the railway bridge,

The ancient whipping post and stocks in Coleshill as pictured in 'Rambling' by J Nigel Hay published some fifty years ago.

to reach a stile in the corner by the river. The Centenary Way is joined at this point. The path bears left, with a fence on the right, until another stile is reached on the right in the hedge.

Follow the Centenary Way by taking a stile on the left, after a few yards, where the H.O.E.W. goes straight ahead. Continue along a surfaced path, with a reservoir on the right, bearing left with the path to find a second, larger reservoir now on the right. Climb the stile ahead (cottage on the right), then turn right alongside the field hedge, from which point there are good views of the second reservoir, still on the right. The path emerges onto a lane which leads to Shustoke village.

Here cross over the main road into Back Lane, almost opposite, with a telephone box on the corner. Continue until a footpath sign points across the 'green' to a corner in front of a bungalow, where a stile leads onto a green track. Continue past a children's play area to cross another stile, then straight ahead on a field path to a cottage, with the path on the left, leading to an exit stile onto a lane.

Turn right and proceed to crossroads. Go straight across to follow a track which leads into a field. Walk with the hedge on the right, then at the far end leave the hedge to go into the next field, bearing diagonally left to the far corner. Cross a stile and keeping the fence on the left continue to another corner stile. Passing a railway house on the left cross a further stile and with the hedge still on the left follow this until a short path on the left leads through undergrowth onto a surfaced track. Turn right to the B4114, then left over Blyth bridge (Blyth Estate is on the right).

After half a mile along the road there is a public footpath sign on the left, leading between houses to a gate on the right. Walk up this field, with a hedge on the right, to reach Coleshill church, then through the churchyard back onto the High Street.

Walk 18

Jaguar Leads the Way

by Ken Rea and his friends

Maps: Landranger 140; Pathfinder 935
Start: Allesley (GR 301806);
Finish: Meriden (GR 252820)
Length of ramble: 8 miles
Transport: WMT 900 bus to the Allesley Hotel
Terrain: Undulating – moderate – mainly fields and woodland
Refreshments: Inns at Allesley and Meriden

FROM the bus stop, opposite the Allesley Hotel, walk back a few yards and turn right into Butcher's Lane, then after a short distance, left into Butt Lane. Continue for approx. 500 yds to a stile on the right, soon after Town Fields Close. Cross to a footbridge, then bear left to a stile. In the next field follow the path uphill to a stile in the corner, then with a hedge on left continue to the Jaguar sports field. Here turn right along the hedge, then left to pass in front of buildings and onto a gravel path. Follow this, turning right to pass tennis courts and onto a drive which leads out onto Brown's Lane.

Turn right here, past a bus shelter, then cross the road and continue to a stile beside No. 212 Brown's Lane. Go down the gully to another stile, then turn right to follow a well-signed footpath through several fields. Eventually the path crosses a stile into an adjacent field and continues on the same heading to go under power lines to a lane.

Cross over to Ted Pitts Lane and walk past houses to reach a junction of paths. Take the left one, passing to the rear of a brick barn and in front of a house to go through a kissing gate. Go straight ahead here through more fields, keeping the hedge on the right, to a lane at Piker's Lane Farm. Turn left for 100 yds, then right over a stile and straight across next field to another stile and footbridge. Here turn right and with a hedge on the right continue to a stile and onto Wall Heath Road.

Cross to a stile opposite, then straight ahead to another stile and footbridge. Follow on the same heading to a gate/stile, then with the hedge on right proceed to double stiles at the top of field, passing and ignoring a waymarked stile on the right. Here turn left to another double stile and straight on in the next field to reach more double gates and a stile. Do not go through these, but turn 90° right, with a hedge now on the left to a stile at the top of the field. *(Good lunch spot here, with open views looking back towards Muzzards Wood).*

After climbing the stile, proceed with the hedge still on the left until it turns a corner, then go diagonally to pass under the power lines to a stile and footbridge. The path follows straight ahead uphill to reach a gate leading to Church Lane. Turn left here and continue down Church Lane until just after a bend and Moor Farm on the right, where a stile leads into a small field. Bear right to another stile and out onto the lane, opposite 'Glen Hellen'.

Turn right for 50 yds, passing a drive to Slashpitts Farm, before going through a kissing gate on the left. Cross a field to the right of a pond and over a footbridge to another kissing gate. Follow in the same direction through two more fields and a gate, then go to the left of a Nissen hut onto a concrete drive, leading to Watery Lane. Here turn

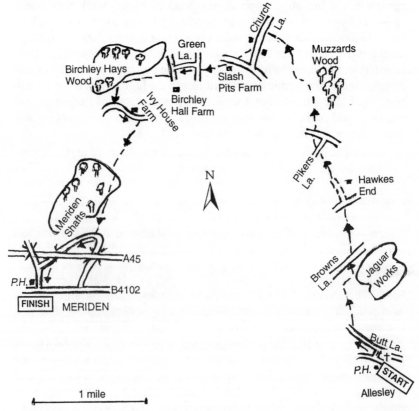

right and after 25 yds left into Green Lane, with its attractive cottages and gardens.

At the top turn left into Windmill Lane, then after 125 yds go through double gates on the right, just before Birchley Hall Farm. Walk along a loose stone track which follows a fence and goes round a left-hand bend to reach a stile hidden in the corner. Turn right to follow the footpath along the edge of Birchley Hays Wood, climbing two stiles *en route*, until a 'Heart of England Way' signpost appears in the right-hand hedge. (*Watch out for deer which may sometimes be seen near the wood in this area*).

Here turn 90° left across the field to a stile and footbridge, then straight ahead to an exit stile onto Harvest Hill Lane. Turn left here and continue on the lane to take a stile on the right, just past Ivy House Farm. Follow the H.O.E.W. down fields to a stile and into trees, turning left onto a narrow track. After about 50 yds turn right over another stile to enter 'Meriden Shafts', a delightful stretch of woodland, noted for its splendid display of bluebells in spring and its autumn colours.

At the end of the wood, a stile leads into a field, where there are a number of horse jumps. Continue straight ahead in the next field to a gate and into Eaves Green Lane. Turn right here and follow this lane for about three-quarters of a mile, forking left and passing under a road bridge, before reaching the Queen's Head at Meriden. After 200 yds the lane joins the B4102 where the bus stop for returning to Birmingham is almost opposite.

The Wesley Tree

by Frances Palmer

Maps: Landranger 139 & 140; Pathfinder 935
Start: Leys Lane, Meriden (G.R. 245820)
Finish: Near Queen's Head, Meriden (G.R. 249820)
Length of ramble: 8 miles: shorter route 6 miles (see footnote on page 73)
Transport from Birmingham: W.M.T. 900 bus to Leys Lane
Parking: Adjacent to Bull's Head and Queen's Head, Meriden
Refreshments: Hotels, Inns and café at Meriden
Special feature: The 'Wesley Tree' (see text)

THE WALK starts at Leys Lane on the B4102 near Meriden Green, traditionally the Heart of England. Here may be seen the remains of an ancient cross, erected in Edward III's reign, also a war memorial dedicated to cyclists who died in the second world war (1939-45).

Bus passengers from Birmingham alight at the stop after Meriden Green, go back a few yards and turn right up Leys Lane, taking the hedged walkway on the left, alongside houses. At the top go straight across the Fillongley Road to a signposted path along 'Green Meads' drive, climbing three stiles *en route* to reach the busy A45.

Here turn left for a few yards, then cross carefully via a 'break' in the central barrier, to a stile immediately opposite down a steep grassy bank. Cross the first field to climb a fence/stile to the left of a metal gate, then with a hedge on the left continue to a gate about half-way along the field and go through this into the adjacent field. Now with a hedge on the right proceed to a stile in the top corner.

From here bear left, keeping to the left of a large oak tree, aiming for a prominent hedge corner, where a waymarked path leads over a stile into a lane near the hamlet of White Stitch. Turn right past cottages and through a gate, then continue to a stile in the left-hand hedge, just past another white cottage. Follow round the right-hand hedge in this field, until at the bottom a footbridge leads onto a woodland path. At the end climb the stile and veer left to reach a cross track, then immediately opposite take another waymarked path through woodland and into a field.

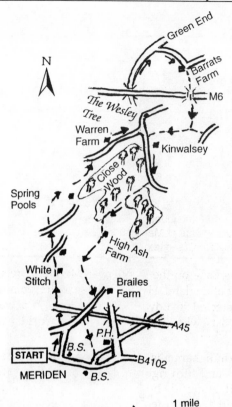

Here turn right for 50 yds to climb a stile in the hedge and continue straight ahead down a long narrow field to another stile in the far corner. Go over this and turn left to follow the hedge boundary to reach a marker post at a gap in the hedge near Spring Pools. Go through into the next field and turn right onto a well defined path for about 50 yds, before reaching a farm cottage on the left, from where a waymarked path strikes diagonally backwards (NNE). This follows a line of telegraph poles to emerge on a lane.

Turn right and proceed along lane, passing Warren Farm, an attractive residence, near which are some ancient oak trees. From here the lane rises steadily to reach a T-junction, where turn left in the direction of the M6 motorway to where the road forks. Here a plaque on the remains of an old oak tree tells us that John Wesley preached under its branches.

(See footnote for shorter alternative route back from here).

The main walk takes the left-hand fork from the 'Wesley Tree' and continues on this lane until a signpost to Green End is reached. Turn right under the M6 road bridge and follow the lane steadily uphill for

---

* *If the shorter route is preferred, retrace your steps from the 'Wesley Tree' and continue on this lane for about a quarter of a mile. Then follow the instructions from ❀ on page 74 to reach Meriden via Close Wood and High Ash Farm.*

The Wesley Tree

about half a mile before turning right again at a sign to Newhall Green. After a further 400 yds take a stile on the right, in a corner by Barrat's Farm, just beyond a stile on the left where the Heart of England Way emerges.

The walk now follows the H.O.E.W. signs for a short distance, turning left over a stile near a barn in the first field, then straight ahead downhill through two fields to reach a footbridge over the motorway. At the far end of the bridge bear left to follow the hedge through two fields and continue around the facing hedge for about 25 yds to climb a stile by a storm damaged tree, then a second stile almost immediately. From here, strike diagonally right across the next field to a gap in the corner near a pool. Bear right and follow the right-hand hedge to another stile, then with the hedge now on the left in the next field, go straight ahead to a stile and plank bridge onto a lane. Here turn left.

❀ Follow the lane for about a quarter of a mile, passing 'Rose Cottage' on the left, until at the end of Close Wood on the right a signpost indicates a right of way. Follow along a well defined track, with Close Wood to the right, and passing a small pool before reaching a stile leading into the wood. The path comes out at the edge of a field, from where another goes straight ahead to High Ash farm.

Here bear slightly right, then left, along the inside edge of the field, keeping straight ahead (due south) with a hedge and fence on the right for about 200 yds to go through a metal gate into the next field. Continue downhill, tree line on right, to climb a fence/stile at the bottom. (There are pleasant views opening up at this point).

Turn right and proceed, passing a small pool to reach another stile, and then continue on the same heading to a further stile and field path, before reaching a tall hedge bordering Brailes Farm. Turn left along the hedge for a few yards, then follow a rather indistinct path through undergrowth which leads to a small field and out onto the road.

Turn right and walk for approx. 300 yds, crossing over the A45 before taking a waymarked path from a stile on the left. Keeping a hedge and stream on the left, follow signs through several fields and a horse paddock to emerge on the main road near the Queen's Head at Meriden. The W.M.T. 900 bus back to Birmingham is from a bus stop opposite.

Walk 20
Shelfield
by Joan Mensing

Maps: Landranger 150 & 151; Pathfinder 975
Start & Finish: Wootton Wawen (GR 148631)
Length of ramble: 7½ miles
Transport from Birmingham: Train (New Street) or X20 Stratford Blue
bus to Wootton Wawen
Parking: Village Hall car park – opposite Bull's Head
Terrain: undulating – easy. (Crops to negotiate during summer months)
Refreshments: Bull's Head pub. and village shop at Wootton Wawen;
King's Head and coffee shop at Aston Cantlow

FROM the railway station at Wootton Wawen take the lane opposite, Gorse Lane, and continue for about half a mile. Just past Gorse Cottage go over a stile on the left-hand side into a field. Keeping to the right-hand edge, follow past a bungalow, to go over a gate on the right, by a pool. Proceed on the same heading to pass a trig point and cross the farm track. At the arrow turn left over a stile and through a gate, then go down the next field, keeping a wire fence on left, to reach a gate. Go through this and with the wood on the right go ahead to a stile at the far end, to the right of another gate.

Turn left on a lane for 10 yards and immediately go over a stile on the

The Bull's Head, Wootton Wawen

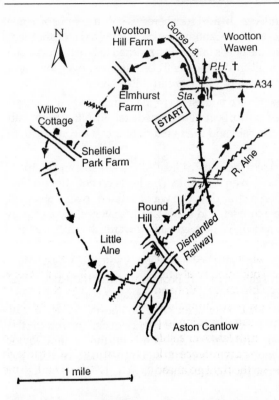

N

Wootton Hill Farm

Gorse La.

Wootton Wawen

P.H. †

A34

Elmhurst Farm

Sta.

Willow Cottage

START

Shelfield Park Farm

R. Alne

Round Hill

Little Alne

Dismantled Railway

†

Aston Cantlow

1 mile

right. Walk straight across the field to pass between farm buildings and a silo on the right. Continue on a wide track to go over a stream, then follow the arrow sign uphill, bearing diagonally right at 240° to the next stile. Carry straight on through fields, with a hedge on the right, over several stiles and through a gate to reach the road at Shelfield.

Turn right here, past 'Shepherds Barn' and continue for about half a mile to a second stile on the left, opposite Willow Cottage. Go over this and straight across the field at 160° to a lane. Climb the stile opposite and continue on the same heading, with a hedge on the right, for a short distance before veering left round the corner of the field to go through a gate. Here, turn right to follow a sign through a copse and into an adjacent field through a gap in the hedge. Turn left and follow with the hedge on the left to the top of the field, before turning left again at an arrow sign. With the hedge now on the right proceed to a stile on the right, cross fields on a due south bearing, following along what remains of a hedgerow on the right and then continue downhill to a stream.

On reaching markers, turn left and keep ahead past beehives, then bear right when the path divides. Cross a stream and then after 100 yards turn right and strike uphill, making for three trees in line, and bear right to a stile at the end of the field, onto a road (Pools Barn Farm sign is on the right).

Cross over and then go straight ahead down the field path opposite, bearing right to go over a footbridge over the river Alne and cross the next field to reach a dismantled railway. From here it is only a quarter of a mile to the pretty little village of Aston Cantlow, which is noted as being the place where John Shakespeare, the poet's father, was married to Mary Arden. The church was originally built in the thirteenth century and over the north doorway an early sculpture of the Nativity can still be seen.

From Aston Cantlow retrace your steps to the dismantled railway and back into the field crossed earlier. Bear right immediately to follow a footpath sign along the edge of the field and then veer right into a second field, to reach a gate onto road.

Here turn left and just past the turn for Great Alne take a stile and footpath on the right, through a field to another stile. This leads up onto Round Hill, an excellent viewpoint on a clear day. The way continues over a stile and downhill to a lane, where turn left and almost immediately climb a stile on the right, in a corner by a farm. Walk diagonally towards the river, keeping it on the right to the next stile.

On reaching a lane, turn right to go under a railway bridge, then immediately go through a gate on the left. Bear right across the field towards the river and follow along the river, passing sewage works on the left. Continue on the same heading, aiming for Wootton Wawen church (one of the oldest churches in Warwickshire, with evidence of Saxon work in the tower and internal arches). The field path leads out onto the Stratford Road, where turn left opposite church, then left again at B4089 to reach the railway station and car park adjacent to the village hall.

The Kings Head, Aston Cantlow

Walk 21
Yarningale Common
by Betty Edmonds

Maps: Landranger 151; Pathfinder 975
Start & Finish: Henley-in-Arden (G.R. 148659)
Length of ramble: 8½ miles.
Transport from Birmingham: Train (Snow Hill) *or* X20 Stratford Blue
Bus (Bus Station) to Henley-in-Arden.
Parking: High Street (Henley-in-Arden)
Refreshments: Haven Tea Rooms (Preston Bagot – on Stratford
Canal); Henley ice cream – a speciality.
Terrain: Undulating – moderate. Steep climbs at the beginning may be
avoided by taking an alternative route beside Beaudesert Mount (* *see*
footnote).

COMMENCE at Beaudesert Lane, alongside the fifteenth century Parish Church of St. John, in the High Street. Near the end of Beaudesert Lane is another church – St. Nicholas, built some 300 years earlier than St. John's, with its Norman arch still in evidence over the doorway.

Where the lane ends, fieldpaths take its place. One of these leads from a metal kissing gate, rising uphill onto the 'Mount' where the twelfth century motte and bailey castle of Thurston de Montfort once stood. After the battle of Evesham in 1265, in which Thurston and Simon de Montfort died, Beaudesert Castle was destroyed and the only visible remains are grassy mounds. The track continues along a ridge, dropping down quite steeply, then up another incline to reach a fence at the top. Cross a fence stile to the right, (electricity pylon in corner), and follow the left-hand hedge to a waymarked stile. From here bear right to a stile in the right-hand hedge, keeping parallel with power lines on left. Climb the stile into a lane, where you turn left and continue along the lane for approx. 200 yds to the second bend.

*   *For an easier route from Beaudesert Lane, follow the grass track to the right of the 'Mount' on level ground to begin with, then rising gradually to reach the fence at the top of the ridge. Here join the main route and climb the fence stile on the right (beside an electricity pylon).*

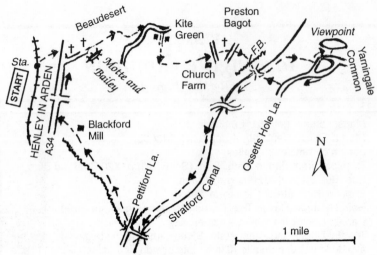

Here take a signposted drive on the right, keeping to the right of a garden to reach a stile. A hedged path now leads past stables into a field. The path goes straight ahead here until half-way down the field, where the route turns 90° left to the hedge and over a stile. Continue now with a hedge on the left, through several fields and over stiles, keeping on the same heading towards a farm. Pass to the left of the farm and eventually through a gate onto a lane. A kissing gate opposite leads onto a narrow hedged track, leading steeply upwards to another kissing gate and out onto the open field in front of Preston Bagot Church. It is well situated and affords excellent views of the surrounding countryside, having been built in Norman times and restored in 1883.

From the church the path crosses a lane to a stile in the opposite hedge. Continue straight ahead to go through a farm gate and turn right to follow the right-hand hedge downhill to a stile. From here the track leads to a footbridge over a stream, then after another 50 yds, over a stile onto the Stratford-on-Avon canal. The building of this canal was completed in 1815 and runs from a point near Kings Norton, at a junction with the Worcester and Birmingham canal, to join the river at Stratford. Characteristic features are its split bridges and barrel-roofed lock keeper's cottages, which add to the charm of this delightful waterway. Much of it has been restored recently.

After crossing the canal bridge go to the left through a metal-barred gate and continue to the left along the edge of a field, with the canal on the left, to reach a stile in the hedge near a corner. A second stile immediately opposite leads into a field, where the path bears slightly

Split bridge on the Stratford Canal

right to pass through a gap in the hedge via a footbridge. In the next field continue on the same heading to a gap in the right-hand hedge, from where the route goes uphill, keeping a hedge on the left. At the top take a stile in the left-hand corner, then follow the edge of a sports field to another corner stile. From here take the main track straight ahead through woodland, veering left across open common to follow a waymarked path, to the right of a Claverdon Council notice. This leads uphill, through a copse, to emerge onto Yarningale Common, a suitable picnic spot, being equipped with seats and affording lovely views of the surrounding countryside.

Leave the Common by taking a track from a horse barrier, which runs parallel with the one used on the ascent and leads back to the lane. Cross this and a cart track to reach Ossetts Hole lane. Turn right onto the lane and continue downhill past a wooded area and a pond on the right, until after about three-quarters of a mile the lane curves to pass Goldson Farm on the right. Shortly after this a wooden post marks the entrance to a short track over a culvert, leading to a gate. From here bear left to a sharp hedge corner, then change direction by turning a few degrees to the right, and walk straight across the middle of field to a gate and onto canal towpath. Turn left to pass the Haven Tea Rooms.

Cross over the road at the next bridge and continue on the towpath, passing near to the beautifully restored Manor House which has been in existence since 1570. Proceed for about 1½ miles, passing bridges 48 and 49. At the next bridge (not numbered), turn right along a farm drive, with cottages on the left, to Pettiford Lane.

Turn right along the lane for about 100 yds, then just past a bridge look for waymarked stile on the left. In the field go diagonally right to a stile in the far corner, then follow alongside a stream at the edge of fields to reach Blackford Mill Farm. After passing a tall hedge on the left turn left to pass in front of the farm house, then right to cross a bridge over a stream. The farm is now a modern residence, but the old waterwheel which was 15 ft in diameter remained in use until 1957.

Follow the path to a stile and into a sports field, where the path goes diagonally right to another stile and out onto the main Stratford Road. Turn right towards Henley, then left at traffic lights into Redditch Road. Almost immediately turn right onto a footpath through a housing estate to reach the railway station. If time permits a walk along the main street in Henley can be recommended, as it possesses a number of picturesque half-timbered houses, including The Old Bell Inn. A delicious Henley ice-cream will complete the day's visit!

Church of St Nicholas, Henley-in-Arden

Walk 22
Little Forde Hall and Mockley Wood
by Les Cartwright

Maps: Landranger 139: Pathfinder 954 and 975
Start & Finish: Danzey Green (GR 123697)
Length of ramble: 7 miles. Shorter version 6 miles
Transport: Train (Snow Hill) to Danzey Green and return
Parking: Danzey Green Station
Terrain: Easy – mainly field tracks
Special feature: Tanworth-in-Arden church and village green
Refreshments: Bell Inn and shops at Tanworth-in-Arden.

O N LEAVING the station at Danzey Green turn left and after crossing the railway take the first lane on the left (Pigtrot Lane). Where the lane turns sharply right take a waymarked track on the left at 'Hard Acre' and continue past cottages for a few yards to a stile on the left. This leads across a field with the River Alne on the left. Follow the waymarked path over several stiles, with the river always on the left, to a footbridge over a stream.

Here the path goes right, with the hedge and stream on the right, until a marker post points left alongside oak trees and a pylon to a stile. Here turn left to reach a tunnel under the railway, then go over another stile and straight across next field to a footbridge. Now follow the left-hand hedge to a sleeper bridge and stile on the left. From here strike uphill, with a hedge on the right, to a stile which leads to the other side of the hedge and continues uphill to exit on a lane to the left of a house.

Turn right along the lane for a few yards, then up steps on the left and through a kissing gate, leading to Tanworth-in-Arden church. This church is of ancient origin, but has been practically rebuilt and was restored in 1881 when it was stripped of its fourteenth century features. On reaching the church a path to the right leads through a gate, where turn left to pass the Bell Inn and the village green. Clustered around the green are buildings that are typical of an English village, namely, a church, school, inn and village hall. The way bears right from the green, then first left into Bates Lane and past the Almshouses.

Where the lane turns sharp left, go straight ahead over a stile, along a green path to another stile, then with a hedge on the right in the next

field to a further stile. From here bear half right to a stile in the far hedge, where take the left of two paths between fences and over a footbridge to an exit stile onto a lane. Turn left along lane, then straight ahead at crossroads to reach a stile on the right, after 100 yds, opposite a bungalow. The path follows along the right-hand edge of a field to a stile and out onto a farm track, then turn left to go through metal gates and a farmyard onto a surfaced road.

Turn left again to reach a cattle grid and kissing gate on right, from where a good path leads downhill, with splendid views across the countryside and Mockley Wood in the foreground. Pass a small pool on the left and well kept grass verges to reach the boundary of Little Forde Hall, a most attractive residence.

You now have a choice of routes – a shorter walk of 6 miles or a longer walk of 7 miles:

SHORTER ROUTE. Turn left to cross a footbridge at a junction of hedges, then left again over a ditch (hard to see when overgrown). Follow a fence on the left, cross a stile and continue to Forde Hall Farm. The path goes through the farmyard and gates onto a tarmac lane, and here turn right past the farm. Immediately after passing horticultural turf suppliers on the left, take a stile onto a field path, adjoining the drive. Go straight ahead with a fence on the left to a sleeper bridge and stile on the left, leading to the other side of a hedge. Turn right, with the hedge now on the right to reach another bridge and stile. Proceed on the same heading, with a stream on the left to a bridge on the left and from here along a bridle track. Cross the railway and through metal gates to a road, and turn left to reach the station at Danzey.

LONGER ROUTE. After crossing footbridges at Little Forde Hall, continue straight ahead, to the left of a stream, over rather rough ground for a short distance, before crossing another footbridge. Follow along a well defined path with a hedge on the right. This was once a wide track, but is now obstructed by trees and often follows the field edge. After about half a mile, passing through a metal gate *en route*, the path reaches an exit stile leading out onto a lane.

Turn right along the lane, uphill to pass Mockley Manor Nursing Home and take a path on the left, a few yards past the drive. After a short climb this reaches a level field, and with a hedge on left to begin with, follow a well marked path, crossing three stiles. In the next field with the hedge now on the right, bear round a right-handed curve to the corner. On reaching the fence, turn left to continue with the hedge still on the right up the far side of the same field (having walked two sides of an irregular shaped triangle). At the top go through a gate onto a track, which passes a wire enclosure where deer are sometimes grazing and leads to Mockley Wood. At this point there is a good view over to the right and on a clear day Bredon Hill and the Malverns can be seen.

Continue straight ahead to go over a stile, from where the path drops steeply down through Mockley Wood, swinging left to an exit stile into a field. Cross to another stile and over a wide bridge which leads onto a bridle path. (The shorter route joins at this point). At a T-junction with another path bear right and follow a rough track over railway bridge to the road, where turn left to Danzey station.

Stiles and footbridge erected by volunteers from Birmingham C.H.A. in conjunction with the Parish Council